HOW TO START Your OWN BUSINESS While Employed

FROM PROCRASTINATION TO ACTION

GBENGA OMOTAYO

Unless otherwise noted, all scripture quotations are from the King James Version of the Bible.

How To Start Your
OWN BUSINESS
While Employed

ISBN-13: 978-1505231564
ISBN-10: 1505231566

Copyright@ 2014 by **Gbenga Omotayo**
www.GbengaOmotayo.com

Published by
Cornerstone Publishing
New York

Phone: +1(631) 894-4584
www.thecornerstonepublishers.com

All rights reserved. This publication may not be reproduced, stored in a retrieval system, or transmitted in whole or in part, in any form or by any means, electronic, mechanical, photocopying, recording, or otherwise, without the prior written permission of the publisher.

Produced in United States of America

Entrepreneurship is a Calling

Are you feeling led by God to embark on the entrepreneurship journey? A Christian entrepreneur is a calling, like any other vocation or profession, where God might want you to serve Him.

DEDICATION

This book is dedicated to my wife, **OLUWABUNMI OMOTAYO,** who has been my "divine helpmeet" as I transitioned into my business. God has given her to me as an anchor, buffer and intercessor. I am very proud to be her husband. My family deserves great applause for being such an encouragement to me.

ACKNOWLEDGEMENTS

I would like to thank my spiritual parents, **Drs. Festus & Anthonia Adeyeye** for mentorship and also for giving me the platform where the seed of this book was germinated.

To **Dr. Tayo Adeyemi** whose ministry played a role in helping me to discover my God-given dream.

To **Dr. Cheryl Hill** who saw clearly the vision of this book and helped in shaping it and to **Pastor Gbenga Showunmi** who first suggested the idea of this book and also is my publisher.

CONTENTS

INTRODUCTION　　　　8

1. The Spirit Of An Entrepreneur..14

2. Before You Quit Your Job..24

3. Exploring Your God Given Business Idea..........................32

4. Validating Your Idea..38

5. Protecting Your Idea...44

6. Creating The Business Plan That Is Right For You...........50

7. Setting Up Properly With The Right Structure.................59

8. Choosing The Right Business Model..................................66

9. Creating & Building Brand Identity For Your Business......75

10. Accounting And Finance Basics For Entrepreneurs.......81

11. Funding Your Business..87

12. Getting Customers..93

13. Marketing Your Business..98

14. Leveraging PR to Build Awareness and Credibility.....106

15. Finding a Business Mentor...110

16. Marketplace Resources...114

ABOUT THE AUTHOR　　　121

INTRODUCTION

You can find studies that show that many people hate their jobs. Some people secretly wish to start a business. People are dismayed with the daily routine, and boring monotonous lifestyle but are afraid to launch out. If ever there was a time to start your own business, now would be it. Entrepreneurs today have access to a wealth of knowledge, a variety of support sources and reduced startup costs.

The spirit of an entrepreneur is difficult to describe because it entails the very core of a man or woman's creativity and passion. My goal is to help men and women fulfill God's calling on their lives by helping them understand the much impact they can make in the marketplace, and to provide spiritual and practical tools necessary to have sustained success.

This book is primarily written as a guide for anyone who desires to start his or her own business. It is written so that individuals can conveniently access educational yet practical content. My aim is to equip leaders in the marketplace, governments and organizations through practical application of biblical principles and ethics.

You will find information that will be easily applicable to whatever phase you are in, concerning your call to entrepreneurship. You will read from experienced leaders in every sphere of influence. This book provides skill development, study, reflection, application and resources. You will be asked to assess where you are, determine where you want to be, and work on the skills and plans to take you there.

Effective Christian leaders should be the "standard" of every sphere of influence. You should be equipped with enough wisdom and understanding needed to achieve your godly vision. As a marketplace leader, you will learn how to take what you receive in the church and apply it to the marketplace (your business).

This book will help you:
- Discover how to make wise decisions and gain a clearer vision and direction for your entrepreneurial calling.
- Develop a concrete strategy and plan to help your business become a reality.
- Develop principles for effective management of people resources.
- Learn how to live with more purpose and passion and help others to do the same.
- Create an action plan to start your business within 100 days.
- If you have already started a business, learn how to fill in the blanks.
- Build and provide quality products or services.
- Generate or raise funding for your startup or business.
- Market and promote your small business, mostly for free.
- Identify, get and keep your ideal customers.

In the Book of Acts 2:17, God says, "I will pour out my Spirit on all people. Your sons and daughters will prophesy, your young men will see visions, your old men will dream dreams."

It is your prerogative to diligently work towards fulfilling the vision God has placed in your heart. Many Christians today are getting daily inspirations from the Holy Spirit on different business ideas and inventions, however due to limited knowledge of what to do and how to go about making this a reality, they lose the drive out of frustration. I believe with this book in your hand, you will turn your own idea into action.

At our various churches and ministries, we regularly get reminded of the need for us to fulfill our God-given purpose and potential, for us to start that business, or achieve that purpose. This is good and very welcome, however the challenge here is that very little is being said or done on HOW we can make this happen. This book will help you overcome the challenges of HOW and fill the void.

The first idea of writing this book came from a good friend, who pastors a church in Texas in one of "our iron sharpening iron moments". He said "Bro Gbenga, you know what? I think you should write a book on **How to Start a Business**".

Lo and behold the following week, my spiritual father and mentor, Dr. Festus Adeyeye, requested that I facilitate a Growth Group for our church members on

"How to Start a Business". You call that coincidence? I said NO!

You may be wondering what qualifies me to write this valuable book. Whatever initial struggle you may have experienced or are experiencing towards fulfilling your business idea, I have been there and am still walking the walk.

I have been through the many phases of transitions; I have been confused; I have struggled, made many mistakes and learned valuable life lessons through hard work. This book will help you to avoid making the same mistakes I have made in developing my God-given business ideas into a visible, viable and sustainable business. I have learned from painful experiences that a business will not succeed without good business practices and principles.

Upon divine instruction received in 2006, Global Christian Event Network (GCEN) was incorporated in New York State with the mission to creating iconic, niche-focused brands that connect and strengthen the faith-based communities they serve. As a leading producer of Christian and community-focused events, such as the Christian Resources Expo and Conference, Night of Gospel Laughs and Platform for Success, I have seen how businesses maximized networking oportunities to fulfill their business goals. Many of the connections made at these events lead to long-term relationships and strategic partnerships.

Also in 2014, I launched Pacetas - A full service Digital

Marketing Agency, which provides integrated marketing solutions to global brands looking to target African niche markets within and outside of the United States. Pacetas is transforming countless businesses in their approach to integrate marketing communications. Also at gbengaomotayo.com, I continue to fulfill my destiny by hosting small group trainings and coaching for many aspiring Christian entrepreneurs. I have the opportunity to speak in various Churches and organizations on topics related to events marketing, marketing communications and business networking.

I believe that at the end of this book, you would have been impacted with knowledge from all my experiences, lessons I have learned, and also the very strategies that assisted me in building some of the fastest growing event brands in the United States.

Strength in Your Work,

Gbenga Omotayo

"To prepare God's people for works of service, so that the body of Christ may be built up." - **Ephesians 4:12**

1

THE SPIRIT OF AN ENTREPRENEUR

"The real reason for my personal and company's existence on this earth, is to give God the credit and to give God the glory for everything good that has been accomplished. God knows how to grow your business in ways you can't conceive. God knows how to coordinate your business in ways you can't fathom. God knows how to orchestrate the overall plan in ways you can't predict or control. Trust Him. And do the work that He puts immediately in front of you to do." — **Bo Pilgrim - Founder, Pilgrim's Pride**

You will find the same thread of evidence in every famous entrepreneur. You will be able to trace it from their childhood to their place of fame. There is a spirit within an entrepreneur that sets him or her apart from others. When, we as Christians, sense this call, many times we believe that it is not of God. We are often displaced by accepting a call to ministerial offices such as Pastor, Evangelist, Apostle, or the like. There is nothing wrong with either calling, but we have to learn to discern the right calling. Entreprenuerial calling exists as well as ministerial calling.

What exactly is it that sets entrepreneurs apart from the rest? What is it that makes certain people believe in themselves enough to risk what we seemingly call "failure" and have the determination to move forward at all cost? It takes an individual who is able to hear from God, set an idea in motion, go through reproach, sometimes shame and ride the waves of the high and low tides of life, at a humble beginning, to ultimate success. This is an ENTREPRENUER.

According to Sarah Pierce, "the entrepreneurial spirit is a gift that inspires others to become the best they can be." Below are five well-known entrepreneurs and what motivates them:

1. Richard Branson - Passion
No one embodies the word "passion" quite like Richard Branson, founder of the Virgin mega brand. Part of Branson's passion lies in his insatiable appetite for starting companies. Founded in 1970, the Virgin Group has expanded to more than 200 companies, ranging from music, publishing, mobile phones and even space travel. "Businesses are like buses," he once said. "There's always another one coming."

Part of Branson's appeal is that he not only has passion for business, but has an incredible passion for life. Branson is famous for his adventurous streak and zest for life, making him one of the most admired entrepreneurs, for his ability to have a successful work-life balance.

2. Jeff Bezos - Positivity

Jeff Bezos knows the power of positive thinking. Living by the motto that "every challenge is an opportunity," Bezos set out to create the biggest bookstore in the world with a little Internet startup called Amazon.

Amazon.com launched in July 1995, and with no press, managed to sell $20,000 a week within two months. By the end of the '90s, though, the dot-com boom had brought Amazon's shares from $100 to $600. To add insult to injury, critics predicted that the launch of Barnes & Nobles' rival website would wipe out Amazon. Instead of hiding in the corner, Bezos came out fighting with optimism and confidence, pointing out to critics all the positive things his company had accomplished and would continue to do.

Bezos continued to expand Amazon, which now sells everything from books to clothes to toys and more. Bezos claims his wife loves to say, "If Jeff is unhappy, wait three minutes." Thanks to Bezos' positive thinking, Amazon.com has grown into a $5.7 billion company.

3. Sergey Brin and Larry Page - Adaptability

To have the ability to adapt is one of the greatest strengths an entrepreneur can have. Every successful business owner must be willing to improve, refine and customize their services to continually give customers what they want.

Google founders, Sergey Brin and Larry Page take this

concept a step further by not just reacting to change, but leading the way. Google continually leads the Internet with innovative ideas that allow people to see and do things in ways they couldn't before (think Google Earth). With their ability to continually be one step ahead, it's no wonder Google is one of the most powerful companies on the web.

4.   Mary Kay Ash - Leadership

A good leader is someone with charisma, a sense of ethics and a desire to build integrity within an organization . . . someone who's enthusiastic, team oriented and a great teacher. All of these attributes were embodied by the late Mary Kay Ash, founder of Mary Kay Cosmetics, a company that has helped more than half a million women fulfill their dreams of owning a business.

Ash's story began as a single mother, working in sales for a home products company. Despite being one of the top sales directors for 25 years, Ash was repeatedly refused the promotions and pay raises her male co-workers were receiving. Fed up with the way she was being treated, Ash started Mary Kay Inc. in 1963 with $5,000.

Ash was best known for being a powerful motivator and inspirational leader, creating a company with a "You can do it!" attitude. Her sometimes over-the-top incentives included the famous pink Cadillac she would give top sales directors. Thanks to her powerful leadership skills, Ash has been named one of the 25 most influential business leaders in the last 35 years, and her company has been recognized as one of the best companies to work for in America.

5.   Debbi Fields - Ambition

At age 20, Debbi Fields didn't have much. She was a young housewife with no business experience, but what she did have was a great chocolate chip cookie recipe and a dream to share it with the world.

Fields opened her first Mrs. Field's store 1977, despite being told she was crazy to believe a business could survive solely on selling cookies. Fields' headstrong determination and ambition helped her grow her little cookie store into a $450 million company with more than 600 locations in the U.S. and 10 foreign nations.

WHAT IS YOUR MOTIVATION FOR STARTING A BUSINESS?

Before you dwell too far into the scary, unpredictable but worthy journey of entrepreneurship, it is very important to settle the question of what is your motivation for starting a business?

Are you starting because you want to make more money to retire on? Get out of the 9-5 bracket? Do you have a genuine passion to meet a need or has God actually called you to do it?

Starting your own business can be an exciting and a blessed experience, but as a kingdom minded Christian ,you want to secure God's backing, as you step out into starting your business. Becoming a successful entrepreneur requires thorough planning, creativity and hard work. For a Christian, starting a business does not just end with the spiritual undertone, but also the real life practical application and relevance.

Every child of God needs to settle it in his or her mind that God desires for us to prosper and have abundance. The platforms God will employ in blessing you are the work of your hand, your ideas and your business. This is why it is very important for a child of God to consider having his or her own business, or at least explore the ideas to see of it is worth pursuing.

CHARACTERISTICS OF SUCCESSFUL ENTREPRENUERS

Consider whether you have the following characteristics and skills commonly associated with successful entrepreneurs:

1. Comfortable With Taking Risks
Being your own boss also means you are the one making tough decisions. Entrepreneurship involves uncertainty. Do you avoid uncertainty in life, at all costs? If yes, then entrepreneurship may not be the best fit for you. Do you enjoy the thrill of taking calculated risks? Then read on.

2. Independent
Entrepreneurs have to make a lot of decisions on their own. If you find you can trust your instincts — and you are not afraid of rejection every now and then — you could be on your way to being an entrepreneur.

3. Persuasive

You may have the greatest idea in the world, but if you cannot persuade customers, employees and potential lenders or partners, you may find entrepreneurship to be challenging. If you enjoy public speaking, engage new people with ease and can make compelling arguments grounded in facts, it's likely you are poised to make your idea succeed.

4. Able To Negotiate

As a small business owner, you will need to negotiate everything from leases to contract terms to rates. Polished negotiation skills will help you save money and keep your business running smoothly.

5. Creative

Are you able to think of new ideas? Can you imagine new ways to solve problems? Entrepreneurs must be able to think creatively. If you have insights on how to take advantage of new opportunities, entrepreneurship may be a good fit.

6. Supported By Others

Before you start a business, it's important to have a strong support system in place. You will be forced to make many important decisions, especially in the first months of opening your business. If you do not have a support network of people to help you, consider finding a business mentor. A business mentor is someone who is experienced, successful and willing to provide advice and guidance.

OVERCOMING YOUR FEAR

Let's face it, one of the top reasons why some people haven't stepped up to start their business ideas is FEAR! Many dreams have been forgotten and buried on the platform of fear. The fact is entrepreneurship is risky, but what isn't? It is always better to do something about your dream and fail, than not to do anything about it. You may be risking success. If you can elevate your faith in God above your fear, you will find out that all things are possible with God.

"I can do ALL things through Christ who strengthens me"
Philippians 4:13 KJV

1. Accept Your Fears and Move On

You know that nagging voice at the back of your head that kicks in with the 'what ifs' every time you are excited about your business idea? What if no one invests in my company? What if no one likes my product and I lose all my money? What if I fail? These thoughts, although normal, can quickly get out of control and affect the way you, not only present yourself, but your small business idea.

Ben Huh, CEO of Cheeseburger, suggests: "Don't fight failure. Take it in and redefine what motivates you. If you can get up over and over again after being knocked down and teach others to do the same, then you can become a person of character, with strong moral values and a rock that can't be shaken. After all, the practice of failure is necessary and never giving up is really the mark of an entrepreneur."

Ben also believes that it's not only okay to make mistakes, it's essential to the long-term growth and success of your company. Why? Because you learn from them – and get better! "And don't avoid talking about your mistakes or fear of failure, because it'll only make things harder on you, and shake your confidence," he said.

2. Fight Fear with Knowledge

There is a measure confidence that comes with knowing your industry, inside and out. It only makes sense, then, that ongoing education, as well as keeping up with the changes and trends in your industry should, be an essential part of fighting your fear of failure.

Susanne Mulvehill of Entrepreneur.com, who started her own entrepreneurial advocacy business, states: "Knowledge is power." Take classes or attend seminars to learn practical skills to start, market, and grow your business.

Not sure where to start? Reading blogs is a great way to stay up to date on your industry. Local community colleges also offer online and in-person courses on various business and computer topics.

Determine the areas in which you feel you could use a little help and then fight your fear of failure by learning all you can about them. This will help turn you into the confident entrepreneur you were always meant to be! I recommend following the blogs of Ms. Willoby, as your virtual mentor.

3. Don't Underestimate Yourself

The reason we underestimate ourselves is often due to a sense of failure through experienced challenges or listening to others that may deflate our sense of self-worth. Challenges create strength, not necessarily by the challenges themselves, but by how we respond to them or how we view the results from them. Do we learn and grow from our challenges?

For example: A challenge may be the loss of a job, spouse or house. The experience may be challenging at first, and bring about all the usual thoughts of loss, sadness, depression and grief. We must realize that we too experience emotional attacks; however, we do not succumb ourselves to the challenge to be overtaken by it. We should look at these situations as opportunities. The opportunities to learn about ourselves and where we may be out of balance in our lives, and ultimately lead to choices that are more in line with our purpose.

2

BEFORE YOU QUIT YOUR JOB

"Suppose one of you wants to build a tower. Won't you first sit down and estimate the cost to see if you have enough money to complete it?" **Luke 14:28 (NIV)**

Starting a business is a huge undertaking that requires so much of your time, resources and commitment. An average company sometimes takes up to 8 years before it can break even, in terms of initial cost investment. Statistics shows that most businesses fail within the first year of establishment. It is therefore crucial that you prepare yourself and get the motive right, before you commence.

Someone once likened starting a business to planting a Chinese bamboo tree, which when planted will not sprout out for the first 4 years, even with daily watering and nurturing, but at the 5th year will grow up to 90 feet tall. What this analogy indicates is that you may spend up to 4 years or more of consistent daily work and business building, and still not break even or be solvent enough to pay your bills. So, adequate planning and preparation is a necessity before entering into the entrepreneurship boat.

Engage In Side Hustle!
My advice is that before you resign your job, try to operate your business as a side hustle, until it can generate your monthly income, or at least something close to it. Instead of taking a second or third job, you should dedicate time to developing the concept or idea of your business properly. If you need to go to school or get trained, use this time to do it. When you carry on your side hustle to a point where you feel you now have a good grasp of the business idea, or you are generating substantial income, or at least have all the necessary tools needed for successful business, and when you know you can no longer handle the pressure of the two jobs, you can then let go of your salary job, to focus fully on your business endeavors.

For example, I operated my business as a side hustle between 2010 to March 2014, before I actually decided to pursue it full time. Was it easy for me operating a business alongside a full time job, as well as family and other commitments? Of course it wasn't easy at all, but the passion to succeed, fulfill my destiny and also break out of the monotonous mundane life of being an employee was just too much drive for me to notice the temporary inconvenience. I used this time of working full time to understand the business, prepare myself and also be able to pay my bills in the interim. I sensed it strongly in my spirit when it was time to move on to doing my business full time. After discussing the decision with my wife, we both agreed to do it and my life has never been the same again.

Even though owning my own business has its peculiar challenges, it also has its peculiar rewards, which in my opinion far outweigh the challenges. My number one benefit is being fully in control of my time. I firmly believe that whoever controls your time controls your destiny. For me, the rewards have not always come in form of more money but in terms of things and opportunities which transcend the value of liquid cash. I have done so much within this short period of time that all the money in this world cannot replace. For example, I have been able to write this book and I am working on two others. My business has enjoyed a level of consistency and I now have quality time to spend with my family.

God Inspired Business Ideas Come in Our Sizes
I know that God will not desire you to start a business that he has not already graced you with the gifting and the ability to do so. Why would God give you desire and love for some things without giving you the platforms and opportunities to fulfill them? God has given all of us gifts, which are things we are very good at. These gifts should have manifested themselves over the course of your life. It should be something that just comes easy to you, something that you enjoy doing.

In 2006 when God spoke to me about connecting preachers and other Christians using the platform of events, it was a good fit for me based on my training, expertise, my passions and desires. I have worked all my life in the arena of events marketing, which makes the call an exciting one for me. Am I saying that all God inspired business ideas will be a good fit for our interests, passions and convenience? No, in some cases, we may be gifted in some areas and have not explored or been exposed to them. So we may not really know if we are gifted in certain areas or not until we actually begin. Therefore, your gifts and abilities may be direct indications of the business ideas he desires for you to work on.

Start Where You Are and With What You Have

In several of my coaching sessions with aspiring business owners, one challenge that stood out among the rest is that of procrastination. It's like they are all waiting for a magical, spiritual or a supernatural hand to push them to write the vision down, create a compelling brand image and start the business. When you have the clarity of what God is asking you to do, you must learn to do something about it, no matter how little or unimportant it may seem. You must start the journey of moving in the directions of your dream business.

I have learned over the years that starting with simple baby steps will give you more clarity on the next step to take. In the kingdom entrepreneurial journey, you sometimes do not see the end result; you walk by faith and as the Holy Spirit directs. In fact, I know so many successful business owners who did not wait to have all the conditions met before setting out. You should perceive when the time is right and seize the moment, when opportunities present themselves.

Dressed In Overalls

Many ideas and opportunities come as challenges. In the words of Thomas Edison, "The reason people miss opportunities is because they come dressed in overalls, or work clothes, and they look like work". To explain further, part of my business is what is called Local Advertising Network, which installs digital screens at restaurants' lobbies. Here people can advertise their products and services. Now, this idea came to me in overalls. Many of my clients always complain of lack of visible results in their traditional advertising efforts. This challenge led me into expanded research, coupled with meditations to seek alternatives. That was how the idea of running digital screen advertisements at various African restaurants came about. Even though it took a lot of work and efforts, today Pacetas Local Ad Network is gradually becoming the most effective singular channel of advertisement for African business owners in the New York Tri - State Area.

Discover What God Has Called You to Do

For most people, what God has called them to do is wrapped up in what they already like to do. Go back through your childhood and reflect on the things you were interested in before you became entangled with life. Find the things that came or come easy and natural to you.

The intersection of what you like to do and what comes natural for you to do is what you are called to do. The problem is that most people know what this is, but they put it aside because someone told them they couldn't make money doing it. Knowing full well that our society does not celebrate mediocrity, I believe you will excel doing what you like and what comes natural because you will do it better than anyone else on the planet.

Get Employed In the Area of Your Calling

Rather than making a choice of employment based solely on financial or monetary gains, you should rather consider skill development, experience, exposure, contacts and expertise in the area of your interest. The best way to do this is by working, interning or volunteering for someone or a company that is already doing it at a high level.

If this happens to be a low paying job, compared to your worth, let it not bother you because you will not be tempted to stay there your entire life. I was able to walk away from my regular 9-5 job, without too much headache, simply because the pay was not too impressive. I personally know many people who have been trapped at their job for years, and find it difficult to leave to answer the call of entrepreneurship, simply because of the attractive salary.

Create another Job for Yourself While Working

While you are working for someone else on a low paying job developing your skills, you should begin the process of creating additional income, based on those skills. For example, I have volunteered, or worked at some projects mainly just to acquire the needed skills. At such times, I have developed my skills on the side as an Event Producer and Event Marketing Consultant. 90 percent of what I am doing today was laid out while working 9-5 jobs.

If You Are Going to Do It, Do It All the Way

In her book Escape from Cubicle Nation, Pamela Slim had this to say, "If you make the decision to leave your job and start a business, do not hold anything back. Throw yourself into it with everything you've got". Social media favorite and TV.WineLibrary.com host, Gary Vaynerchuk threw out some motivating concepts for aspiring entrepreneurs at a Web 2.0 Keynote conference in New York in September 2008 that are worth repeating:

- Stop doing what you hate! Gary's slogan is the sum of Jim Collins's advice to "find out what you are genetically encoded to do" plus Gary's concept of "Hustle 2.0." Basically, once you know what work you can "kill at," do it full out, every day, until you make it a viable business.

- Work your face off! Gary is not one who believes in working four hours a week to launch a business. He advocates doing whatever it takes to grow your brand, connect with your customers, and monetize your business, even if it means working on your side business from 9 p.m. to 1 a.m. for a year or two.

- Stop watching episodes of "Lost"! Despite feeling like there is no extra time in the day, many people waste time on pursuits like cheesy television shows and meaningless Twitter conversations. If you want to make your business happen, you will have to be ruthless with your time.

- Legacy is more important than currency. How

do you want to be remembered by your children and grandchildren? Will they be more excited by their grandma who diligently trudged into her cube at 7:58 each morning and clocked out at 5:00 or by Grandma 2.0, with strong opinions, passions, and an unwavering dedication to making a difference in the world?

3

EXPLORING YOUR GOD GIVEN BUSINESS IDEA

"He has filled them with skill to do all kinds of work as engravers, designers, embroiderers in blue, purple and scarlet yarn and fine linen, and weavers—all of them skilled workers and designers". – **Exodus 35:35 NIV**

So the next important question now is how do you receive a business idea from God? Or how do you know for certain that this consuming nagging and persistent idea is God given or worth pursuing? Or how do you know the heart of God concerning the plans? Well, Proverbs 20:5 says, *"Counsel in the heart of man is like deep water; but a man of understanding will draw it out."*

Based on the understanding of this verse, we can safely conclude that for us to actually download business ideas and innovations from God, we need a vibrant growing and continuous relationship with Him by seeking His presence and meditating on His words. We cannot afford to stay too far from the Holy Spirit, who is our ever dependable ally.

According to Dr. Jerry Savelle, "Hunger for God and a deeper revelation of his words are the keys to receiving God-given opportunities and God ideas. His ideas come to us through his wisdom of God, through his word and through his spirits speaking to our hearts."

GOD GIVEN IDEA PROGRESSION FORMULA

In Amos Johnson's book, "Take Control of Your Financial Destiny," He spoke about the 3 Step Idea Progression Equation that God will take you through by which your passion is transformed into a business. The first step of the Idea Progression Equation is **wisdom,** second **understanding**, and the third is **knowledge.** Whether God has spoken clearly and directly to you about an idea or you have experienced the process I just described above, what you need to do is run your idea through this 3-step process that I personally use all the time, and have recommended to some of my students, and they have outstanding results.

1. **WISDOM FROM GOD**
*The LORD by wisdom hath founded the earth . . . **Proverbs 3:19***

When God put an idea into your spirit either through dreams, visions, inner witness, word of knowledge, encounter or trance and so on, it is generally given in the form of wisdom from God. This wisdom is a general direction of what needs to be done but without specific details and actions to be taken in achieving it. For example, in 2006 the Holy Spirit told me to "connect churches and ministers using events as a platform in preaching the gospel of Jesus Christ" This is a classical form of the wisdom of God, which in itself was somehow challenging for me to execute, even though it appeared direct and straightforward.

There were various options and ways I could interpret these words of wisdom, which is where you have to be very careful in not jumping to start something without further clarity from the giver of the idea. In my own case, I stumbled several times because after hearing the word of wisdom, I excitedly started making elaborate plans of logos, names and many more, without further clarification, as well as seeking the understanding and knowledge needed in making accurate decisions.

As previously mentioned, you sometimes may not have heard an audible voice or conviction from the Holy Spirit about an idea. You can however subject your thoughts under the direction of the Holy Spirit for clarity and direction.

If God gives an idea or inspiration to one, it is surely to meet a specific need. I am positive that God will not grant you an idea in a vacuum, so be very conscious not to run ahead with a God inspired idea, without first knowing what needs it is meant to meet, who the targets are supposed to be, and what form the products or services should take.

Oh Wait. But God did not speak to me expressly? Does

that then mean that God will loudly speak into our ears these ideas and innovations? Not necessarily and not in all cases. As a child of God, I believe that you do not have to have heard clearly in an audible voice or dramatic encounter to know if is God speaking. I believe this is an area where some of us are getting it wrong.

If you are a child of God, whatever idea that comes to your spirit, which is recurring, persisting, and unshakable, and when scrutinized in the light of God's word, does not negate or contradict your faith, watch it closely. God may be saying something here. If the business idea you are thinking about aligns with your passion, life purpose, direction; correlates with your experiences and validates your skills, then this is an indication that God may be leading you in this direction, even when you did not hear an audible voice.

If you desire to start a business and are yet to hear or receive a specific idea, your first step is to find a profitable business idea. According to Marlee Ward of Radical Entrepreneurship, there are two ways to do that:

1. Pick an idea from an existing or proven business model.
2. Find a need in the marketplace and fill it.

Making money in business boils down to one thing: Providing a service or product people are willing to pay for. Your job is to find out what that thing might be. And it becomes easier, if you are focusing on your strength areas, because it's never easy building a business you have no skill or interest in.

HOW CAN YOU KNOW?

Search forums
When you're searching forums, look for the things people are complaining about. What types of problems are they discussing? What are they telling fellow forum members about what they want or wish they had? If you discover enough people griping or desiring the same thing, you could be very close to finding a product or service people would pay for.

Search Social Networks
Search Facebook and LinkedIn groups related to your niche of interest. Use Twitter search to find people talking about your area of expertise.

Conduct Keyword Research
Once you've gotten a feel for the kinds of problems, needs, and desires you want to address, use Google Keyword Planner to get an idea of how large your target market could be. Generally, you're looking for phrases that point to buying behaviors.

Talk to people about their problems. Nothing replaces the power of getting real-time human feedback on problems, needs, and desires people would pay to have addressed.

2. UNDERSTANDING
Having received an idea either directly through the Holy Spirit or through systematic research and due diligence,

you must meditate on the wisdom (high level concept) you received until you have faith in the wisdom. This is called understanding, which anchors the idea in your heart "... *by understanding hath he [God] established the heavens.*" **Proverbs 3:19**

This verse points out that understanding creates the foundation of the idea. In the case of the earth, the heavens are the foundation of the earth, and with a house, the foundation is the ground it is established on. When your faith is built up concerning the business idea, then knowledge is released to make accurate decisions on the action steps to take.

"By his [God] knowledge the depths are broken up, and the clouds drop down the dew." **Proverbs 3:20**

3. **KNOWLEDGE**
Finally, after you have understanding, which comes after your faith has been built up on the wisdom you received, God will begin to give you systematic knowledge on a need-to-know basis; instructions on how to move forward with the idea. This usually comes as inner conviction, intuition and an assurance of what the next step should be.

At this stage, you should begin to answer vital business questions such as what is the business concept, who would be the ideal target customer, where would they be located, what is their buying behavior, how is the market structured, what would be the best model to use and so forth.

4

VALIDATING YOUR IDEA

"Quaker Mill was struggling; I brought my business problems to the Lord, something that was very unusual at that time in Christianity. An idea came to me that was to change breakfast tables forever. Up to that point, oats were presented for sale in big barrels or boxes, set on the floors of grocery store. I envisioned Quaker oats on grocery store shelves in individual, sanitary, cardboard containers. The idea worked. Demand soared." **Henry Parsons Crowell – Founder Quaker Oats**

Having received clarity of the idea through the spiritual process described above, it is time to make it applicable and see the viability and practicability of the idea. Here are five steps for doing that:

1. Check for Profit Potential

Identify people or businesses doing the type of business idea you have and see how profitable it is for them. Most often than not, there should be some competitors in the market, which indicate a ready market waiting to receive your idea. The lack of any visible competitor may mean either the business idea is not realistic or God may be taking you to a totally virgin land and giving you the first mover advantage. Search Google, Amazon or Craigslist and all the social media platforms, to identify businesses already in your target market.

2. Determine If Your Target Audience Is Large Enough

One of the easiest ways of doing this is to use the Facebook Ad Manager inside Facebook to accomplish this. Pretty much every demographic is represented on Facebook with over a billion active users. With the Ad Manager, you can know the approximate number of users that fit your target market, based on your given demographics. Knowing the size and reach of the specific group your product or service will serve will help you decide if this would be viable, in terms of profitability or not. You do not want to spend time, money and resources building a product around a certain segment and later realize it is not large enough to be profitable.

3. Determine How Much Your Product Or Service Would Cost

Identify a price range that would be consistent with your pricing strategy and target audience, as well as with the going rate for your offer and go with it. Your price will probably change once you create and implement your offering anyway, so it's not a huge issue at this stage. Setting a price for your product or services at this level will help you determine if you can make profit doing this business. To determine how much money you could make serving 1% of the market, use your estimated total market size, multiply that figure by 1%. Then take that number and multiply it by your price.

Here's the formula:

ETM x 1% = Total Annual Sales (TAS)
TAS x YOUR PRICE = Gross Profit
Whatever outcome you get should be a number you are comfortable with and if not, you may not have a viable business idea after all.

Is that a number that would make you profitable after one year of sales, having accounted for both fixed and recurring expenditures that would be deducted as well? If not, you need to consider if you've got too small of a market, too low of a price, or a bogus idea. If you're thinking that 1% is an overly conservative estimate in sales, you're right. If you've got a ripe market, you'll likely sell more than that.

4. Test Your Idea

Now, you just need to know, will people actually buy your product or pay to use your service? This is a really important step in the process because people will tell you they want to buy all day long, but when it comes to time to pay, their wallet stays in their pocket. Testing your offer is the only surefire way to know if you've got something worth committing to.

Test your idea online. One of the easiest and most effective ways you can test your idea online is to create a simple landing page that presents your offer to prospects. For example, while I was still writing this book, I had already created a landing page for it at www.gbengaomotayo.com/thebook. There are two ways to do this. You could actually send people to a page that asks them to buy. Then, when they click on the "buy" link, explain that the product/service is not available yet, but for access to the product/service (at a discount) have them submit their name and email address.

Now, you're doing three things. **(1)** You're verifying that people actually want to buy. **(2)** You're building an email list, and **(3)** You're lining up future sales. Or you could drive traffic to a landing page that asks if the prospect would like to learn more about the offer. The data from this testing isn't as strong as the prior example, because it's not requiring a buying decision, but if presented properly, it's still a good indicator.

Explaining how to run ads for testing or learning about creative landing pages that sell for you before you even build your product is beyond the scope of this book, but if you want to learn how to do these, you should visit my website www.gbengaomotayo.com and sign up for one of my free courses.

5. Consider Crowdfunding

Widely known as platforms to raising money for businesses or projects, crowdfunding is also a perfect platform for testing the viability of your business idea because people are actually giving you money to get it off the ground. It is common sense to know that if people are donating money overwhelmingly to your idea, it is an indication that the same people would be willing to pay for it, when it comes out. There are tons of crowdfunding platforms available. Check the chapter on funding for an exhaustive list of available crowdfunding websites.

6. Ask Similarly Situated Businesses If They Would Be Willing To Offer Your Products Or Services

Offering your products or services to businesses that offer complimentary products or services to the same target market is the single fastest way to build a customer base (and test the value of your offering). If you make the arrangement sweet enough for the participating business (make sure it benefits them in some way) they can get you instant exposure to a buying audience. This arrangement can be referred to as cross selling in marketing, where products or services are offered as a bundle package. Having another business offer your product or service is almost like an endorsement of your offer.

THE IDEA CHECKLIST

These are questions you should ask yourself to help screen and stimulate your thinking and also clarify, as well as streamline, your ideas.

- Can you for certain say this was divinely revealed to you?
- Does your idea solve other people's problems?
- Do a lot of people have this problem?

- Are you passionate about this idea?
- Are you willing to commit the next 5-10 years of your life to this idea?
- Who are your competitors?
- Can you do something substantially different or better than others?
- Can you build the business on your capital resources?
- Could you have products and customers in 90 days or less?
- Do you have a background and skill set compatible with this business?
- Do you have competitive advantage on how to get customers?
- If you don't start this, will someone else?
- Can you court mentors who have been successful doing something similar?
- Does the business risk / reward match your personal risk/reward?
- Does it help you fulfill your purpose?

5

PROTECTING YOUR IDEA

"He is known for spending thousands each year to advertise in newspapers the Gospel during the Christmas and Easter holidays, to playing Christian music in his stores and closing on Sundays. Green reasoned, God is not averse to business, he's not just a Sunday Deity and he understands margins, spreadsheets, competition and profits. The message prominently displayed in my childhood home was, Only one life; 'twill soon be past. Only what's done for Christ will last." **David Green, founder of Hobby Lobby**

As God has given you this unique idea, made to measure business idea or innovative product, it is very important that you take all precautionary measures in protecting it from predators out there. God holds you accountable for your destiny. There are several ways you can protect your idea from being stolen or imitated. One of the first things I did with "Night of Gospel Laughs" was to trademark the name and the logo image in the US with the US Copyright commission.

The government has provided the platform to defend intellectual property, which is generally the ownership of something intangible, such as an idea, design, concept or formula.

There are Four Major Ways of Protecting Your Idea

1.	Copyright: Work of authorship (literature, source code, musical composition) US Copyright Office.
2.	Trademark: A sign or indicator associated with a brand (logo, slogan, brand images): Trademarkia.com.
3.	Patent: A work of invention (a machine, process or physical products): US patent & Trademark.
4.	Trade Secret: A process or formula that retains value by remaining secret (example coca cola): Non-Disclosure Agreement.

WHEN TO SHARE YOUR IDEA

Sometimes, due to the nature of the idea or business God has revealed to you, it is very important and necessary to share with others. Either share with family members for encouragements or suggestions, or share with professionals, such as lawyers and accountants, for services. It is however very crucial to take precautions against it being stolen or duplicated easily.

It's natural to fear that your idea might be stolen. But you can't turn your vision into reality without the help of others. Sooner or later, you're going to want to ask an industry expert to evaluate your product or service. You're going to need to collaborate with a manufacturer or distributor.

Not sharing your ideas through fear will hurt your business because it will keep you from getting feedback from others. When you bring your idea up with someone new, they give you their own thoughts, which in turn helps you grow your concept. By never discussing your business with others, you miss that chance.

WAYS TO PROTECT YOUR IDEAS

1. Pray and Listen to the Holy Spirit
"When the Spirit of truth, comes, he will guide you into all the truth." **(John 16:13)**

Sometimes you feel uneasy about doing business with some people or sharing the idea with them. Always listen to your inner voice and the Holy Spirit. The proverbs remind you to trust in the Lord with all your heart; do not depend on your own understanding. Seek His will in all you do, and He will show you which path to take.

There was an acquaintance of mine who offered to assist in taking one of the events I produce to the next level. I was excited because he is highly respected and successful. During this time, he kept asking me for the template, the blueprint and other sensitive info concerning the event. I didn't have any peace about this partnership arrangement and prayed about it. One night, while I was sleeping, I had a few seconds trance and his picture came and right there I heard the voice of the Holy Spirit not to do it. That incident saved me a lot of agony and the rest, as they say is history.

2. Non-Disclosure Agreement (NDA)

An NDA is a simple written document to be signed and returned to you. It can be a mutual agreement between two parties not to share information with third parties, or it can go one-way (since you're sharing information about your idea with them). If the agreement doesn't have an expiration date, that's powerful. However, it's important to note that many investors will balk at signing an NDA before you speak with them. Since the balance of power is in their favor, this may be something you'll have to give up, if you want investors. The same holds true for potential clients. Instead of requiring a signature, consider simply printing a confidentiality statement on your business plan.

3. Do Your Research

Before you begin working with anyone new, be it an individual or organization, do some research online. Do they have a good track record? Can you find any complaints about their business practices? If you find cause for concern, consider changing your mind or pray more about it. Things are not always the way they seem. Just typing a name accompanied by complaint on Google has saved me lots of heartache and thousands of dollars, in the past.

4. Non-Compete Agreement

If someone works with you, have him or her sign a non-compete agreement. A non-compete agreement prevents an individual or entity from starting a business that would compete or threaten yours within an established radius.

5. Work-For-Hire Agreement

If you hire someone to help fine-tune your product, make sure to establish that you own any and all improvements made to the idea. Anything they come up with, you own. You will still need to list the person who came up with improvements as a co-inventor in your patent, but they will have no rights to your invention.

6. Avoid Revealing Too Much

One of the best ways to secure your idea is to only reveal what is absolutely necessary. If you're pitching an idea to a potential client, give only the details necessary to convey the idea. It's not necessary to share every detail of how your product works.

7. Apply for a Provisional Patent

A patent can incur far more expenses than a startup is able to pay. During the process of shopping your idea around, a provisional patent can protect your idea for the first year. After twelve months, the provisional patent expires, however, with no option of being extended.

8. Trademark Your Name

A trademark can provide an additional layer of protection, since a company's name is often tied closely with its idea. Also, by establishing a trademark, you also have added protection, in the event a legal issue should arise. The documentation required to register a trademark can serve as written proof that your business idea was in the works, at a specified time. These dates will be crucial in establishing the exact date your idea was in the works, in the event that someone else tries to dispute this fact.

9. Document It

Put as much in writing as possible and save that documentation. By creating a paper trail, you'll have proof of your concept, if it does go to court. Keep a log of every discussion you have where details of your business are disclosed. This log could come in handy, if you find one of those conversations go somewhere. You can download sample templates at www.gbengaomotayo.com.

6

CREATING THE BUSINESS PLAN THAT IS RIGHT FOR YOU

"And the LORD answered me, and said, write the vision, and make it plain upon tables, that he may run that readeth it." **Habakkuk 2:2 KJV**

BUSINESS PLAN DEMYSTIFIED

There have been a lot of misconceptions and misrepresentations, when it comes to writing a business plan; above all, it has discouraged a lot of small business owners from attempting to prepare one. At the end of this chapter, I hope to have successfully shown you how to create a business plan that is right for your business.

Due to the varied requirements of businesses, the business plan also has different composition. Someone leaning towards borrowing money or sourcing investors would create more in-depth plans than someone who is just starting out with their own seed capital and with a low entry capital or startup.

Many intending business owners do not understand the importance of having a business plan. It is in YOUR best interest to complete a succinct and simple plan for your business because it has many benefits of going through a business planning process, but here are some of the main reasons:

Clarity
Most people have some kind of plan in their head anyway. Putting it on paper helps you make that plan crystal clear!

Objectivity
A business plan helps you stay objective and allows you to take a professional look at your business.

Focus
A written plan will help you identify objectives and focus on what needs to be done in both the big picture (strategies) and the daily activity (tactics).

Accountability
When you have a plan, you can refer to the plan to make sure every action being taken supports the overall plan.

Prioritization
Your plan will help you with priority setting, and will help you look forward to where it is you are going, so you can be clear about the steps you need to take next.

Opportunity Identification
A business plan also helps you identify opportunities

when they appear. Specifically, the plan will help you recognize which opportunities are on the path and which opportunities can be passed on.

Effective Decision Making
A written plan helps you make effective decisions that are in alignment with the objectives of your business. For example, when opportunities are presented to you, you can say YES or NO, depending on whether it fits your plan. You may even add an item to your plan because the new idea/opportunity fits your overall business objectives.

You should also determine why you want to write a business plan. Some important reasons are:
- To evaluate initial startup costs.
- To establish the fundamental viability of a project.
- To define your products, services and customers and assess competitors.
- To map out the business model, the goals and the strategy used to achieve them.
- To communicate to others (banks, investors, partners, etc.) the business idea.

WHAT IS A BUSINESS PLAN?

Your business plan is a simple, straightforward, written plan that answers the following 5 questions:

1. What kind of business am I building? What is my VISION?
2. Why am I building this business? What is my MISSION?

3.   What are the results I am going to measure? What are my OBJECTIVES?
4.   What will make this business successful over time?   What are my STRATEGIES?
5.   What is the work to be done? What are my ACTION PLANS?

1.   **VISION: What am I building?**
What business are you creating?
What will your business look like in one year, three years and five years?

a) Company Name: (What is the name of my small business marketing company?)
    Example: Pacetas: A Full Service Digital Marketing Agency

b) Location: (Where will my business be located?)
    Example: New York, USA

c) Services: (What services will my company provide?)
        Example: Small Business & Startup Coaching, Workshop & Seminars, Event Marketing, Small Business Advertising, Digital Marketing Services. Also Branding, Graphic Design, Social Media Marketing, Email Blast, Web Design, Video & Event Production.

d) Specific Audience: (Who am I providing these products and services to?)
    Example: Aspiring entrepreneurs and existing small business owners within the Christian faith based community.

e) 1 Year Metrics: (What are the specific metrics to know I am successful?)

Example:
$50,000.00 of revenue and 20 individual clients to go through our educational programs, and an ongoing service relationship with at least 5 small business company clients.

NOW: Put all of your answers into the following VISION Statement template:

Within one year, I will grow (Location) based (Company Title) into a (Revenue Goal) business, which provides (Specific Audience) (Services) helping over (Clients helped).

Example:
Within one year, we will grow New York - based Pacetas Agency into a $50, 000 dollar business, which provides Small Business & Startups Coaching, Workshop & Seminars, Event Marketing, Small Business Advertising, Digital Marketing Services for Christian ministries, small business and startups.
– helping over 20 individual and 2 big company clients.

2.   MISSION
Why am I building this business?
Why does this business exist?
Why am I starting this business, and what is the purpose?
What promise am I making to my clients?
What is motivating me to build my company?
What is my unique mission?

What promise do I make to my clients?
What gets me excited about what I am doing?
What inspires about what I am creating?

Examples:
Pacetas Agency is committed to helping startups, small businesses, not-for-profits and aspiring entrepreneurs with cutting-edge marketing tools. We help individuals reach their highest personal and business potential by discovering and developing their God-inspired ideas into profitable business ventures that glorify God.

3. OBJECTIVES

What are the results I am going to measure?
List your overall objectives by outlining your most important business goals, making sure that your goal is S.M.A.R.T compliant. That is to say, it is Specific, Measurable, Achievable, Realistic, Time Bound).

How will you measure success in achieving your goals?

You must be able to track your objectives. This means you need exact numbers that can be monitored for accountability, motivation and success celebration!

Example #1: Enroll at least 100 individuals in our Starting Your God Inspired Business with Ease by Oct 2015.
Example #2: Complete two full 2-month Tele-trainings by Dec, 2014.
Example #3: Write and send 10 online newsletters by Dec, 2014.
Example #4: Conduct 4 individual train-the-trainer 1-day consultations by Dec, 2014.

Example #5: Lead 2 LIVE presentations on other people's stages by Dec, 2014.

4. STRATEGIES
What will make this business successful over time?

Key Questions to Address
1. Write down your business strategies by answering these questions:
2. How are you going to build your business?
3. What will you sell/ what is the product?
4. What is your unique selling proposition (i.e., what makes your business different from the competition)?
5. What's the market opportunity? What problem are you solving? How large is the market opportunity? How many dollars are spent on it every year? How fast is it growing?
6. How will this idea make money? Is it a subscription service, or do you sell one-off products? Do you make money on ads?
7. What is your long-term strategy? Where do you see your company in 5, 10 or 15 years? What are the key metrics to hit?
8. How will you sell or market your products? How will you get customers?
9. What is the total startup capital you will need to launch your business?
10. Who is your team? Why are your skills are uniquely qualified for this business?
11. What are the prices for your products?

12. What do you estimate your business' ongoing monthly expenses will be immediately after launch, in

three months, in six months, and in one year?
13.   What do you anticipate your business's ongoing monthly income will be immediately after launch, in three months, in six months, and in one year?

5.   ACTION PLANS

What is the work to be done? Create an action plan by answering:
- What are the specific action items and tasks you need to complete now?
- What are your future milestones?
- What will need to be accomplished by those milestones, in order to meet your objectives?

Examples:
- Develop publicity & marketing plan by 2/28/2015.
- Develop "Starting Your God Inspired Business" webinar series by 3/31/2015.
- Contract w/Audio Designs for CD production by 6/30/15.
- Submit articles to Inc., Entrepreneur, and Home Based Business for Dec. publication by 7/31/15.
- Complete mailing to 250 trade associations by Sept. 1st for 2015 speaking engagements.
- Complete "Easy to Implement Marketing Tools" CD by 10/31/2015.
- Complete "How to Start Your God-Inspired Business" book by 12/31.

SUMMARIZE (ONE PAGE PITCH)

On a single page at the beginning, list the main points of you plan in bullet point form. Write this summary last, but put it at the front of your plan.

If you would like to learn how to create a practical step-by-step business plan beyond the scope of this chapter, head over to gbengaomotayo.com

TIPS: Keep your business plan short and simple!

7

SETTING UP PROPERLY WITH THE RIGHT STRUCTURE

"If you have anything or if I have anything, it's because it's been given to us by our Creator; I don't care if you're in business or out of business, God owns it," You can't have a belief system on Sunday and not live it the other six days."-
David Green, Hobby Lobby CEO

Now that you have developed a Holy Spirit-assisted plan that is appropriate for your type of business idea, which you are very comfortable with, your next step is to set up your business with its own life and form. The Bible reminds us to write the vision and make it plain, and since that has been done, it is time to make it come alive by following the plan already written down.

CHOOSING THE RIGHT STRUCTURE FOR YOUR BUSINESS

Your business must have a structure and a form. There are many forms of business structures out there. Some have been in existence since the beginning of business, while the advent of the Internet is bringing in more and more.

Each of the common structures has its own pros and cons, however the type of business you intend to start will determine which one you should go with. In setting up a structure, as a small business owner, you must consider the following FOUR factors in making a decision on which structure will better meet your immediate need:
- The potential risks and liabilities of your business.
- The formalities and expenses involved in establishing and maintaining the various business structures.
- Your income tax situation, and
- Your investment needs.

There are various known structures available to businesses; notable are the sole proprietorship, LLC, S & C Corporations and partnership. Each of these has its own advantages and disadvantages.

LLCs are the most common business entity for Entrepreneurs. Of all the business entities, a limited liability company (called an "LLC") is the most common for entrepreneurs just starting out. An LLC is a legal entity, which in the eyes of the law, exists separate and apart from its owners, just like a C-Corp and S-Corp.

Also, just like the "C" and "S" corporations, an LLC offers limited liability from obligations of the business, and owners are protected from personal lawsuits (unless they committed a criminal act) against the actions of the business.

An LLC, although a business entity, is a type of unincorporated association and is not a corporation. The primary characteristic an LLC shares with a corporation (C or S) is limited liability, and the primary characteristic it shares with a partnership is the availability of pass-through income taxation.

Why a Common Choice?
- LLCs offer greater flexibility in ownership and ease of operation.
- There are no restrictions on the ownership of an LLC (unlike in S-Corp).
- An LLC is simpler to operate because it is not subject to the formalities by which C-Corp and S-Corp must abide. For example, in most states there is not a requirement to hold annual general meetings for shareholders.

Pass through Taxation
Entrepreneurs setup S-Corps in order to benefit from the fact that profits and losses pass through to the owners' personal tax returns. This is helpful when you have loses, because you can reduce your taxable income. Well, the LLC allows you to do the exact same thing. With an LLC, all profits and losses are passed to the members' personal tax returns.

Self-Employment Tax
A disadvantage of an LLC is that all earnings are generally subject to self-employment tax. By contrast, earnings of a C-Corp or S-Corp, after paying a reasonable salary to the shareholders working in the business, can be passed

through as retained earnings, which are not subject to self-employment taxes.

Very Flexible

Now, what makes an LLC outstanding is that you can avoid paying self-employment taxes on retained earnings. When you first setup up your LLC, by default, all profits are taxed as normal income and subject to self-employment taxes; however, LLCs are eligible to apply to the IRS to be taxed as a corporation. If you make this election, you avoid paying self-employment taxes on retained earnings. I really like how flexible the LLC is!

WHEN AN LLC MAY MAKE SENSE

For the majority of small businesses, the relative simplicity and flexibility of the LLC makes it the better choice. This is especially true if your business will hold property, such as real estate, that's likely to increase in value. That's because regular corporations (sometimes called C corporations) and their shareholders are subject to a double tax (both the corporation and the shareholders are taxed) on the increased value of the property, when the property is sold or the corporation is liquidated. By contrast, LLC owners (called members) avoid this double taxation because the business' tax liabilities are passed through to them; the LLC itself does not pay a tax on its income.

WHEN A CORPORATION MAY MAKE SENSE

An LLC isn't always the best choice, however. Occasionally, other factors will be present that may tip the balance toward a corporation. Such factors include the following:

1.	You expect to have multiple investors in your business or to raise money from the public. While an LLC works fine when you have just a few investors -- especially those who will be active in the day-to-day operations of the business -- it may get more awkward when the number of investors increases. For example, you'll likely run into resistance from potential investors ,if you can't offer them the corporate stock certificates that they consider tangible evidence of their partial ownership of the business. Rather than wasting your time trying to overcome this resistance, it's probably better to structure your business as a corporation.

2.	You'd like to provide extensive fringe benefits to owners. Often, when you form a corporation, you expect to be both a shareholder (owner) and an employee. The corporation can, for example, hire you to serve as its chief executive officer, pay you a tax-deductible salary, and provide fringe benefits, as well. These benefits can include the payment of health insurance premiums and direct reimbursement of medical expenses.

The corporation can deduct the cost of these benefits and they are not treated as taxable income to the employees, which can be an attractive feature of doing business through a regular corporation. With an LLC, you can only deduct a portion of medical insurance premium payments, and other fringe benefits provided to members do not receive a favorable tax treatment.

3. You want to entice or keep key employees by offering stock options and stock bonus incentives. Simply put, LLCs don't have stock; corporations do. While it's possible to reward an employee by offering a membership interest in an LLC, the process is awkward and likely to be less attractive to employees. Therefore, if you plan to offer ownership in your business as an employee incentive, it makes sense to incorporate rather than form an LLC.

WHEN AN S CORPORATION MAY MAKE SENSE

Self-employment taxes can tip the balance toward S corporations, since LLC owners may pay more. What are self-employment taxes? Well, you know that taxes are withheld from employees' paychecks. In 2014, employers must withhold 7.65% of the first $117,000 of an employee's pay for Social Security and Medicare taxes, and 1.45% of earnings above that amount for Medicare taxes alone. The employer adds an equal amount and sends these funds to the IRS. (The total sent to the IRS is 15.3% on the first $117,000 of wages and 2.9% on anything above that.) You may not be aware that the IRS collects a similar 15.3% tax on the first $117,000 earned by a self-employed person and a 2.9% tax on earnings above that amount. This is the self-employment tax.

For an S corporation, the rules on the self-employment tax are well established: as an S corporation shareholder, you pay the self-employment tax on money you receive as compensation for services, but not on profits that automatically pass through to you, as a shareholder.

If you have decided on going with the sole proprietorship, here are the action steps to take:

WHEN A SOLE PROPRIETORSHIP MAY MAKE SENSE

Sole Proprietorship is the easiest, simplest and the least expensive form of business structure. In New York, you can establish a sole proprietorship without filing any legal documents with the New York State Government. There are five simple steps you should take:

- Decide on a desired business name (more on this later).
- File a fictitious name certificate with the county clerk's office. It is called a "trade name," "fictitious name," or "doing business as" (DBA).
- Obtain licenses, permits, insurances and zoning clearance. For example, lawyers, doctors, masseuses, chiropractors, architects and many more vocations require a state board to examine and certify them. Visit op.nysed.gov to apply for a license.
- Obtain an Employer Identification Number.
- Apply for a business bank account. Bring your certificate of assumed business name to the bank, along with other identification, and open a bank account.

There is no right or wrong structure to adopt; each one has its own merit and limitations. Let your individual circumstances and the nature of your business determine what structure to adopt. In any case, whatever structure you go with will most likely be between a Sole Proprietorship, LLC and Corporation, due to their ease, popularity and tax breaks, respectively.

8

CHOOSING THE RIGHT BUSINESS MODEL

"Making money to be your goal will lead you to poverty but focusing on serving the public, your employees and your vendors leads to prosperity"- **David Steward, Founder Worldwide Technologies**

According to Wiki definition, "business model is the rationale of how an organization creates, delivers, and captures value." Consistent with this definition, we see the business model as the explanation of how a firm translates an idea into value, or more bluntly, into money. According to Peter Weill, it generally consists of two elements: (a) what the business does, and (b) how the business makes money doing these things.

The same way we have various structures so do we have varieties of models for business. The advent of the Internet as well as globalization has brought about newer models of business operations. As mentioned earlier, you should not make a decision of what form of model to adopt based on popular opinion or directions, nor should it be based on sentiments but rather on the most suitable and appropriate format that fits perfectly your situation.

Here are the most common business models, among which I hope you will find an appropriate one for your business operations

1. Home Based
Working from Home. This is probably the most cost effective business model that is fast gaining popularity. This model is suitable for those whose business does not require or has limited physical interactions with customers. Businesses such as website designer, digital marketing etc. do not require a visit to carry out an assignment. Most often, when contracts need to be signed or a physical contact is required, the meeting can be set up at a local restaurant, breakfast bar or even rented office space for as little as $5 an hour. Gone are the days where businesses working from home are looked down on; now they are looked upon with admiration for boycotting paying unnecessary expenses that go with office rentals. If your business falls within those described above, or you are just starting out, this may be your best option.

2. Bricks-and-Clicks Model
This is a hybrid of the shopkeeper/ office front and e-commerce model, in which a company integrates both offline (bricks) and online (clicks) presence. It is also known as click-and-mortar, as well as bricks, clicks and flips, with flips referring to catalogs. It's great for big

companies like Wal-Mart, BestBuy, Shoprite but not a good choice for startups.

3. E-commerce

This model is suitable if your business is selling products online such as Amazon and EBay. It's the electronic version of a catalog and shopping cart, and today rarely involves any stock of product. Products are usually drop-shipped directly by the manufacturer. Your major investment is on the initial e-commerce website development and the periodic maintenance. This model is suitable for someone with little or no capital to start a business.

4. Shopkeeper (Brick and Mortar) Model

This is the most traditional and successful approach in use for centuries. It implies setting up a store in a location where potential customers are likely to be, with products and services on display, being sold at some multiple of cost to cover the overhead and realize a profit. Despite its widespread success in the past, technology has made it much easier to do this type of business without the rigors and extra setting up costs associated with this business model.

5. Franchising

According to Franchising.com, franchising is a "hybrid" form of business model in that it combines aspects of a sole proprietorship with those of a corporation. Franchising allows a business owner to grown a business by selling the rights to use their brand and business model, instead of building new units on thier own. A franchise can be a good way for a novice entrepreneur to get started because he can follow a successful business blueprint.

In a franchise operation, the owner of the original business, known as the franchisor, essentially sells the rights to use his brand to an entrepreneur called a franchisee. The franchisor provides the franchisee with ongoing support in areas such as business operations, marketing and obtaining financing. In return, the franchisee agrees to follow the franchisor's business model and to pay the franchisor royalties based on a percentage of unit sales.

According to the Entrepreneur website, franchisors may paint an overly rosy picture of franchise ownership to entice franchisees to take the plunge. Talk to other unit owners to get a realistic idea of what to expect before purchasing a franchise. Examine the franchise agreement closely so you gain a clear understanding of your rights and obligations.

Get More Information
If you are considering purchasing a franchise, FTC's Bureau of Consumer Protection has a wide range of resources and guides to help you buy a franchise and avoid franchise taboos. SBA also has available on its website over 30 blogs covering franchise tips and best practices. If you would rather have a one-on-one consulting or wish to learn more about how I can help you through this process, head over to gbengaomotayo.com to subscribe to one of my e-courses.

69

6. Subscription Or Licensing Model.

This is consistently becoming more popular as business operations, protocols, service delivery and many more are being turned to autopilot, with the aid of technological advancement. There are automated services that you can incorporate into your business core operations, simply by signing up for monthly payment, to enjoy all of the benefits of such services.

With this model, all you have to do is pay a contracted price to have access to the product or service on a periodic basis (monthly, yearly, or seasonal). The model works online, offline, through magazines, newspapers, and television. The advantage is recurring revenue, without finding new customers.

7. Multilevel

Multi-level marketing (MLM) is a marketing strategy in which the sales force is compensated, not only for sales they generate, but also for the sales of the other salespeople that they recruit. This recruited sales force is referred to as the participant's "down line", and can provide multiple levels of compensation. Other terms used for MLM include pyramid selling, network marketing, and referral marketing. According to the US FTC, some companies that use multi-level marketing exploit members of their networks and constitute illegal pyramid schemes.

Notable companies using this model include Amway, Tupperware, Herbalife, Avon, Mary Kay and The Pampered Chef. Salespeople are called independent business owners (IBO) and generally work from their homes.

On the surface, it's hard to tell the difference between a legitimate MLM and a pyramid scheme. That's because they're both built on the business model of "multiple levels" of distributors and recruits. Some critics of MLMs claim that all of them, even the supposedly "legitimate" ones, are pyramid schemes in disguise. Some people are passionate about it in the extreme, and there are even top celebrity authors like Robert Allen, Mark Victor Hansen, and Robert Kiyosaki doing it and advocating it. Yet, in many circles, it is a taboo to mention being a network marketer.

My honest advice is that you should check it thoroughly before you decide to join. Personally, I prefer to take the time to focus on what God is calling me into than to use all my energies in developing a business that I do not have a long-term stake in, nor does it have any bearing to my life goals and passions.

8. Iron Sharpens Iron business strategy

Look for businesses that are serving your target market except what you have. To better understand this model, think of the word "symbiotic" – like a parasite, only mutually beneficial and generally non-destructive. Another way of looking at it is offering complimentary products or cross-selling with another well established brand or company.

A great example of this is one of the events my company currently produces - Christian Resources Expo +

Conference which, in the middle of year 2014, adopted this model. The success of the expo depends on having a large gathering and turnout of the targeted audience attend the event. We are overcoming this challenge by partnering with other Christian events, such as summits and seminars with little or no interest in exhibition. This arrangement has successfully marketed the New York Empowerment Summit. The arrangement is a huge blessing to both organizations with a win-win outcome.

There are countless ways we can leverage on each other to promote ourselves for less. However you need to make sure that the host is better off partnering with you, instead of just adding that product to their own offerings. Otherwise you'll lose your business the day they realize they can offer the same thing themselves and make more money.

In his study of 1000 largest US firms on the topic "Do Some Business Models Perform Better Than Others?" **Peter Weill,** in a 2004 MIT paper, argued that all businesses could be classified based on what rights are being sold. From these rights, 16 distinct business models emerged, where any business can be classified as one or a combination of these models.

For relevance to the audience and the scope of this book, I will briefly explain three of his business models. My advice is for you to take the time to research organizations using any of your preferred models, to learn more about their failures and strategies for success.

Model 1: The Developer Business

This model typically is used to create a business with the intention of selling that business to someone else for profit. So, from the word go, your intention is to create something out of this world that would be so revolutionary and challenging to the status quo, to the extent of it being attractive to bigger organizations. There is Dr. Dre's Beats Electronic acquired by Apple for $3 billion. According to the co-founder with Dr. Dre, Jimmy Iodine, "I've always known in my heart that Beats belonged with Apple. The idea, when we started the company, was inspired by Apple's unmatched ability to marry culture and technology. Apple's deep commitment to music fans, artists, songwriters and the music industry is something special." Another great example is Nigerian, Chinedu Echerio's Hopstop, that was acquired by Apple for on estimated $1 billion.

Model 2: The Inventor Business

If you like to create, but not sell, then this model may be what the doctor ordered. With this model, you create products and have them legally protected; i.e. a patent or copyright. After the product is protected, the rights are then sold to a manufacturer and the product is sold to another company. The inventor only creates the idea or prototype, but hands it off to other companies to mass-produce and sell. This is one of my favorites that I recommend to Christians whom God is giving creative ideas every day but do not have the resources to make them happen. There are several companies out there such as INVENT who would basically help you take the idea to full production, without you spending more than the registration fee of less than $500.

Model 3: The Contractor Business

This is probably the most common business model for first time entrepreneurs. In this model, you sell a service provided primarily by individuals, such as consulting, construction, education, personal care, package delivery, live entertainment, or health care. Payment is in the form of a fee for service, often, but not always based on the amount of time the service requires.

Remember that your area of gifting already has all that you need to make it happen. This discussion relating to business models is here for your information, so you know where your business is positioned in the big scheme of things. You should therefore not make a choice of business models based on popular culture or what you feel most comfortable with, but it should be based on whatever you think is right for your business success.

9

CREATING & BUILDING BRAND IDENTITY FOR YOUR BUSINESS

"A born again Christian, Strive Masiyiwa, was quoted as saying that he reads his Bible for at least 4 hours a day – if he's busy! He tithes 10% of his annual income to his church. Together with his wife, he personally pays the school fees for over 22,000 Zimbabwean orphans. God will do nothing except you pray; and you have to be clear what you want." - **Strive Masiyiwa, Founder Econet Wireless**

Now that you have taken the time to analyze and decide on the best model to use in launching your business, it is time to assign physical attributes and presence to your business. Without a good brand image and identity that perfectly presents your idea in a way that it would have the right appeal and connections with your desired audience, succeeding at the business will become a challenge.

You see, owning your own business represents a lot of positive and interesting things but the core of it is having a profitable and sustainable business. You cannot have a sustainable successful business without first having to build a solid and consistent brand identity; a brand image that is consistent in the mind of your customers and a promise that is clear.

Just like many business newbies and aspiring entrepreneurs, and despite my marketing degree, I used to think branding is so much of the logos, colors, images and all that, but over the years I have learnt that building a good brand goes beyond doing just that.

WHAT EXACTLY IS A BRAND?

According to Seth Godin, a brand is the set of expectations, memories, stories and relationships that, taken together, account for a consumer's decision to choose one product or service over another. If the consumer (whether it's a business, a buyer, a voter or a donor) doesn't pay a premium, make a selection or spread the word, then no brand value exists for that consumer.

Based on the above definition of what constitutes a brand, I have therefore highlighted the critical steps you should take in building a sustainable brand. These steps should be followed through even before you contact a graphic artist to develop your brand identity (logo, business card, use of colors, font, website etc.)

1.   Write out your entire customer experience. If a brand is the set of expectations, memories, stories and relationships that, taken together, account for a consumer's decision to choose one product or service over another, it then makes sense to predetermine these memories, stories, expectations and customer experiences. Therefore write out what that experience should be from the moment that the prospect finds you all the way to when they received what they paid for. Include all the steps, the little details and every action taken.

2. **Identify your promise.** In addition to the customer experience, you would like to identify the promise that you want to make to your customer. So, your promise can be made up of a number of things, or it can focus on just one thing. In any case, whatever it is, ensure that it is crystal clear. For example, your promise may be to deliver a service within a certain number of days or to provide a "waoh!" service by surpassing customers' expectations.

3. **Weave your promise into your process.** Now you're going to look for ways to build that promise into your experience. So, for example, let's say that one of the promises that you want to make, as a book publisher is to publisher, any book within a certain number of days, as it was the case with my publisher: www.thecornerstonepublishers.com. In its marketing material, it promises to publish any book in 30 days or less and they actually did. So, they have taken the time to break down the 30 days to ensure that every key task, such as proofreading, editing, layout, cover design etc. is completed in record time, to be able to keep that promise.

Also maybe you're a graphic designer who promised to deliver a design that accurately represents the client's expectation. Then you want to make sure that, in every step in the process of design, you are meeting that promise. One of the ways that you may be able to do this is by having a very in-depth questionnaire that asks them all the questions that will be necessary for you to get a good solid concept on the kind of design you need to create. Perhaps that could be followed up with a phone consultation, where you cover the things in that questionnaire, to make sure that you have more clarity. And then, you might want to offer three complimentary revisions that are included in your design project, so that you can tweak the design to make sure that you're really meeting those specifications. That means you're meeting your promise at every single step.

4. **Match your promise and your design elements.** Match your promise to the creative aspects of your business. So, this is where the logo, color scheme, and design really do come into play. Make sure that those things that you select truly reflect whatever promise it is.

5. **Keep your promise consistently.** Make sure the promise is executed over and over again. If you make a promise to deliver high quality products and services in an efficient manner, then make sure you're doing that over and over again. Because it's in consistency with your promise that you will gain a positive brand image and build the brand equity you need for your brand to carry you through your business long term.

6. **Register a Business Name and Secure Online Presence.** Based on the vision God has given you, what is your business concept? What is the name of the business

and its tag line? Also, you should be able to express the business concept in one simple sentence. It is really important for a brand name to be attractive, simple and short, so that the targeted audience can easily remember it.

In "The Art of the Start," Guy Kawasaki recommends some guidelines for choosing a name:

- Have a first initial that's early in the alphabet (you will be in a directory, may as well be in the top).
- Avoid numbers (too hard to know how to spell: 1 or one?).
- Pick a name with "verb potential" (think Google).
- Sound different (don't choose a name close to a competitor or other, unrelated brand which will get confusing).
- Sound logical (match your business name with what you actually do).
- Avoid the trendy (probably not a good idea to call your firm Sick and Phat Technology Services).

In the online world, it is equally important to have a domain and social profile names available for your brand name, or else your efforts might help some other company or brand. One good resource to use in searching and securing your online space and social media addresses is http://namecheck.com/ (Domain, Facebook, Twitter, Instagram, Pinterest, and LinkedIn). Just type in your preferred name or domain and it will instantly generate a result across all platforms telling you which is available or which has been taken.

7. Design Logo & Company Identity (Business card, Letterhead, Envelopes, Phones). At this point, you should be able to decide on a color and brand logo concept consistent with the image you are projecting to the public. You can either contact a professional graphic designer or a branding company like ours - www.pacetas.com and we do a pretty good job too. Or you can use crowd sourced websites such as **Odesk** to let professionals design your logo or use websites like designmantic to make your logo yourself and get it instantly.

8. Build a Website and Develop Your Social Media Platforms. If you are done with the logo and stationery for branding, now it's time to have a good looking responsive website that can please your targeted audience, as well as search engines.

You will have multiple options available and you can choose any but if you are looking for a choice without investing much in it then crowdsourcing is a way out! If you are a bit tech, you can get a WordPress template and build your website yourself

10

ACCOUNTING AND FINANCE BASICS FOR ENTREPRENEURS

"For which of you, desiring to build a tower, does not first sit down and count the cost, whether he has enough to complete it? Otherwise, when he has laid a foundation and is not able to finish, all who see it begin to mock him, saying, 'This man began to build and was not able to finish.'" **Luke 14:28-33 ESV**

Having a well thought out financial plan is an important component that should be incorporated into your business. In fact, sponsors and investors consider this section to be the most important in your entire business planning process.

HOW TO PUT TOGETHER A FINANCIAL PLAN

The first thing you should do is to carry out a thorough research and audit of your financial needs, as it relates to you and your business as a whole. There should be a proper analysis and description on the cost of production, as well as all of the associated cost, in terms of marketing strategy and other organization operating principles to be put in place.

Every conceivable item that pertains to your business as an expense should be defined before you set out to create your business financial plan. The goal is for you to be able to operate your business on a predefined budget, so there are no hidden or undefined costs that may threaten your business operations over a certain period of time.

When you have a good picture of how much money you would need (both fixed and recurring expenditure), you should make provision for at least six-to up to a year cushion. This is a good place to start, but how long you'll need a cushion depends on what business you are in.
This cushion would be the same amount you would need to take care of not only your personal expenditure, but also all of the costs associated with the business.

KEYS TO FINANCIAL PROJECTIONS

To have a workable and relevant financial plan, you must make calculated assumptions and projections on income statement for the future.

There are 5 steps to take:

STEP 1: Estimate your one time start-up costs and recurring monthly expenses. This is represented as Operating Expenses + Cost of Goods.

A. Knowing Your Startup Cost:
List what you think your company will require just to

open its doors. Research the price of each line item. If you are unable to obtain the exact price, use a conservative estimate. These expenditures may include legal fees, professional fees, licenses and permits, advertising and promotion, consulting, stationery, logos, letterhead, rent before start-up and insurance before start-up.

After totaling your expenses, you may come up with a figure that seems frighteningly large. If so, revisit the list and decide which are absolutely necessary and which are more discretionary. Eliminate those you can do without and obtain at a later date.

Even after trimming expenses, the amount of money you may need may be beyond the scope of mere savings. That's where loans come in. But the key is to borrow just the right amount.

B. Know Your Operating Overhead Costs:
Think about how much the company's day-to-day operations will likely be. As you did with the first step, list all the expenses you feel will be necessary to keep your doors open. These often include your salary, all other salaries and wages, rent, advertising, delivery expense, supplies, telephone, maintenance and professional fees.

STEP 2: Figure out your balance sheet. This will be a snapshot of your current assets and liabilities, in relation to one another. Project your balances per month, forward to one year.

STEP 3: Figure your income statement. Also known as your P&L (profit and loss). This will be a measurement of your total cost against your total revenue to determine your net income. This too is also projected monthly forward to one year.

STEP 4: Figure your cash flow projected per month, forward to one year. A cash flow statement is a financial report that describes the sources of a company's cash and how that cash was spent over a specified time period. Some of the sources to consider will be salaries (if currently employed), operations, loans etc.

STEP 5: Include your current personal financial statement, if you are applying for a loan. A lender needs to know your personal net worth based on obligations and other personal debt.

Now Summarize Your Current Financial Overview Using Excel spreadsheet, capture the following:
- Your Income: all sources of current income.
- Your Expenses: average monthly spending.
- Your Savings: how much liquid cash you have saved.
- Investment: how much do you have in investment account.
- Debts: total outstanding debts.
- Employee Benefits: health insurance, retirement, sick pay, vacation etc.

BREAK-EVEN ANALYSIS
The break-even analysis indicates what will be needed in monthly revenue to reach the break-even point.
- Projected Profit and Loss
- Projected Cash Flow

- Projected Balance Sheet (assets & liabilities in relations to each other)

KEY PERFORMANCE INDICATORS

This is the progress of your business based on some key indicators. It varies from business to business but generally the following metrics should be used to measure your success:

1.   Number of customers at a given moment or period of time.
Growth rate: How many customers you have gained over a period of time.
2.   Total Sales: sales made at a period of time.
3.   Expenses: expenses incurred in total on operations and cost of goods.
4.   Customer rating: ratio 1-10

SUMMARY

- Income Statement (Profit & Loss Statement): Measurement of your total cost against your total revenue to determine your net income.
- Gross Revenue: Total amount of Money Company brings in.
- Cost of Goods: Cost of materials to develop your product.
- Gross Profit: Gross revenue minus the cost of goods.
- Operating Expenses: Everything supporting the business outside of cost of goods like rent, salaries, marketing etc.
- Net Income: The actual revenue you're left with

after goods and operating expenses, the true measure of profit.

KEYS

- The two key programs that you must learn, as a small business owner, for bookkeeping and tax planning are QuickBooks and Excel.
- Excel: Use to calculate all the financial statements.
- QuickBooks: Helps with accounting for the long term.
- Track spreadsheet for finance.
- Clean your credit, reduce your expenses and build cash reserves.

11

FUNDING YOUR BUSINESS

Jesus said, "Where your treasure is, their your heart will be also." Tom has been extremely successful in business while sticking to his Biblical values and using his influence to further the Gospel. When asked his thoughts on money, his response was, "Money is not evil, as so many people think. It pays for Bibles and churches and hospitals." - **Tom Monaghan- Founder, Domino Pizza**

Funding for your business idea would probably be one of the challenges you may face in your entrepreneurial journey, unless you have adequately prepared yourself or have figured out a way in advance. In your financial planning, the first thing you want to do is carry out an extensive research to identify how much funding you would need and for how long. This would take into considerations all of your initial startup cost, as well as your recurring expenditure, and so forth.

In my experience, I believe you will fare better if you

can totally avoid borrowing any money whatsoever and work with what you have on ground. Ideally, you should have been able to save or place some funds aside, or been procuring most of what is needed to effectively start upyour business, such as website and other needed tools for business operations.

When you take off like this, with a short-term plan, you will have more clarity, as the businesses progresses, on which direction to channel your efforts. You will be able to test the waters to determine if you really want to do this, or if your focus is right, and where to really spend money. At the end of the short-term plan, (maybe 2 years) you will have more insight as to how to move forward, and when you secure funding at this stage, you will be better prepared to spend it wisely.

WHEN YOU HAVE LITTLE OR NO CAPITAL

What if you do not have any money or have any available option? Should you stop or place the vision on hold? I once listened to a message by Pastor Sam Adeyemi of Daystar. According to him, he did a research throughout the Bible and there was no single place where God had to use money to start or create anything. All God had was a thought and an idea of a good thing and he called them forth by speaking. He concluded that we do not have a money problem but an idea problem. If the idea is well received and conceived, the resources will be made available.

According to Chris Guillebeau, author of the $100 Startup, "To succeed in a business project, especially one you're excited about, it helps to think carefully about all the skills you have that could be helpful to others and particularly about the combination of those skills."

a. Make Something
Create your product yourself and upload it online to sell. There are websites with millions of traffic from across the globe, such as eBay, to consider as platform.

b. Resell Something
Many people have made millions just by becoming a reseller on websites such as eBay, shopify, amazon etc. Create an online account, upload you products and set up partnership with a drop shipping company who would take care of all order fulfillment, without you doing anything yourself (and they take a percentage off each unit sale).

c. Sell Your Services
One way to start a business with little to no startup capital is to sell your services, instead of a physical product. There are a huge variety of services you can offer, depending on your background and interests. Because you are selling your services, you will need a branding plan to make sure your name and company get in front of the people who may need the service. Some places that are free for promoting your services include Fiverr, Craigslist, Elance, Taskrabbit and Skillshare.

It's also useful to have a website to show samples of your work, list your experiences, and blog about your industry, to draw visitors. If you want to learn more about branding and online marketing beyond the scope of this book, you can visit my website www.gbengaomotayo.

com for the e-course on this topic.

d. Barter To Get What You Need
I have created free marketing campaigns in exchange for introductions to some high net worth clients, and I have also done some free consultations in exchange for legal consultation. The options are endless; think of what you can offer for free to someone in exchange for what they also can give you for free.

e. Utilize Low-Cost Services
As mentioned previously, you can use sites such as Fiverr or Elance to advertise your projects. Web design can be as cheap as $100 and graphic design can be done with less than $5.

FUNDING SOURCES

Five Funding sources I recommend in the order of preference:

1. Personal Line of Credit
A personal line of credit is the first option to self-fund a business. It's very much like giving yourself a loan, a little at a time. It can be a good option for a modest size business that is expected to have recurring costs over its start-up and early operational phases. If you have any money set aside, through savings or inheritances or whatsoever, it is good to utilize it but make it out to your company as a loan, so as to allow your business to work hard at repaying it. I prefer this option the most because if you are really serious about owning or starting your own business, you should have at least been saving up or keeping some funds aside towards it, which proves how

serious you are towards your goal.

2. Crowdfunding

The practice of funding a project or venture by raising many small amounts of money from a large number of people, typically via the Internet. This approach, not only helps you in raising funds, it also helps you in testing the validity of your idea and also pre-selling it. These are some of the crowdfunding platforms available out there:

1. Faith Launcher
2. Give for Christ
3. ian d700
4. WeRaise.us
5. Indiegogo
6. Crowdfunder
7. Rockethub
8. Crowdrise
9. Somolend
10. appbackr
11. AngelList
12. Invested.In
13. Quirky
14. Kickstarter

3. Friends and Family/ Angel Investor

This is an investor who provides financial backing for small startups & entrepreneurs. Angel investors are usually found among entrepreneur's family and friends. Your first set of optimists and cheerleaders would mostly come from your family, who would be willing to support you and see your business succeed, even if it means not getting their money back.

4. Small Business Finance

Small business finance for start-up operations can be obtained from the Small Business Administration (SBA) in the form of a loan. Typically, you'll need a business plan and some form of collateral. The loan is done through a bank that works with the SBA and usually has a lower interest rates. . http://www.sba.gov/loans-and-grants

5. Bank Loan

Business loan from a credit union or bank works very similar to an SBA loan, except you don't have the government involved and may need to pay a higher or standard interest rate. This can make the lender a little more reluctant to make a loan, but if you have a good business plan, then I wouldn't worry about it. The lender will want to make certain you have collateral or some demonstrated way of paying back the loan.

12

GETTING CUSTOMERS

"Famous for living on 10% of his income and giving 90% to the spread of the Gospel, LeTourneau exemplified what a Christian businessman should be. RG thought that anyone who was wholly committed to Christ had to become a pastor or a missionary to truly fulfill the great commission. After deep prayer with his pastor, RG LeTourneau was shocked to hear Rev. Duvol say the words that guided him for the rest of his life, God needs businessmen too." **RG LeTourneau – Earthmoving Innovator**

Scholars and leaders of thought have stated that, as a startup, getting customers should be your number one priority and that you should spend at least 50 percent of your time getting customers, at least for the first 6 months. However the reality is that you may neglect these core activities, if you do not properly manage your time. One of the greatest challenges you would face, as a small business owner, is that of time management. Your time is your life and your money, you alone are expected to carry out all of the myriads of roles necessary for business success, such as sales, marketing, PR, promotions, phone calls, accounting and record keeping, among others.

SALES, MARKETING & P.R

You should know that your success as a startup depends largely on three key area of business: funding, product development and acquiring customers. This chapter is dedicated to the third, Acquiring Customers, and I will discuss the areas of business activity that directly affect your customer acquisition:
- Sales: The actual exchange of value
- Marketing: Getting people interested in that exchange of value
- PR: Building awareness and legitimacy around your product/services (value)

HOW TO MAKE SALES

Whatever product or service you desire to sell, there are generally 5 basic steps necessary to conclude a sale. However, there may be a little variation with the sales process between a Business to Consumers (B2C) and a Business to Business (B2B) company, which requires more process and sometimes slower decision making procedure due to the many organizational structures and hierarchy.

5 STEPS TO SALES PROCESS

The first thing to do is obviously to introduce yourself, your business (product or services) in the form of emails, phone calls, or face to face meetings and then book a meeting.

1.   Gain Interest: In your attempt at selling your product or service, you should start with what people are mostly interested in - THEMSELVES. If you can focus on them, maybe a compliment or interest in them, you will gain their attention, which would give you the platform to then sell anything.

2. Establish Credibility: To cultivate trust, you must establish a sense of credibility through past accomplishments or experiences that justify your competence and the ability to sell the product or your services. These are achievable through showing word of mouth, testimonials, building referral system and making reference to past transactions.

3.   Establish Need: If you cannot establish why they need your product or services, it will be difficult for you to sell anything effectively. You should carry out a research of your prospect's needs ahead of the meeting and show them how you can help them meet that 'need' or solve the problem. Through listening, empathy, and affirmations show them clearly their need, whether they know of it or not.

4.   Offer Solutions: Once the need is clearly established, offer your product or service as the solution, but do not push it. Show them clearly how your product or service can help meet this established need.

5.   Have Systems For Easy Transaction: Many businesses have lost sales, due to difficult or slow transaction processes, and this can be a major barrier to making sales. Make your sales transaction processing simple and effective either through online system, telephone or in person. Always be ready to process payment. In this day of progressing cashless system, there are various systems that allow you to process credit card payment or over the phone on the go.

PROSPECTING

Since it is not everyone that is in need of what you offer, and also considering your limited resources of time, money and personnel, it is important for you to prospect and screen every potential customer, to know who to dedicate your limited resources to. Therefore prospecting is a process of discerning who your potential customers are and designing a flow to reach them with your products or services.

CREATE A SALES FUNNEL

To effectively prospect, you will need to create a sales funnel. A sales funnel is an inverted pyramid that draws potential customers through a company's sales process. As the name indicates, it is wide at the top because customers with all levels of engagement enter and eventually the strongest leads are channeled to the bottom, to be turned into successful sales, using the sales process.

Golden Rule: 1 out of 10 people will buy your product So if going by this rule, we must ensure that our sales funnel needs to be wide enough. So if you want 10 customers, you reach out to 100.

COMPOSITION OF A SALES FUNNEL

Top of the Funnel: Everyone enters here, possibly as a result of the interest generated in your product through an effective marketing or promotions strategy. The top of the funnel is the widest because no filter mechanism is at play, and there is encouragement for everyone to explore.

Middle of the Funnel: At this stage, a customer has taken a step beyond just going through basic information regarding your product. This minor initial commitment tags them as a sales lead. It means that something about your offering moved them beyond just observing to actual action, albeit a minor gesture. Each one will be assessed, based on their level of engagement or attractiveness. This is a tricky stage because there is access to a wide variety of expressions of interest, and identifying potential sales correctly can make the difference between successful sales and wasted efforts.

Bottom of the Funnel: A potential client (sales lead) at this stage is someone who is qualified and ready to make a purchase. This assessment is based on their degree of interest, based on observing how they behave. If they have made repeated inquiries, shown repeated expressions of interest etc., then they become an opportunity. A client at this stage is ready for a proposal or personalized pitch, to allow them to formally commit to your product.

13

MARKETING YOUR BUSINESS

"Any faith-based business owner should always pray to get guidance. Before I create a card, I pray about it and I pray to know what I should write. What's the purpose of this card? What I've seen in my business is a pattern; where there's stress, it's followed by a blessing."- **Scott Osborne of SentForHim.com**

Getting people to show interest in what you do is critical to having a successful funnel, which you can prospect and get your 10 percent out of it.

CREATE A MARKETING PLAN

Traditional marketing plans widely circulated are not designed with much consideration for small business owners and aspiring ones, as yourself, but for venture capitalists who require a lot of details before they can make a decision whether to release their funds or not. It is just too complicated and inapplicable. The following steps I am about to share with you have been developed through years of consulting for small businesses and used by many leading consultants to better help you have a vibrant marketing plan that works.

Here are four processes to having a vibrant marketing plan:

1. Situation Analysis: (Where You Are)
Here you should give a little background of your marketing efforts, where you are, your challenges and any other details. It should not be more than one paragraph or so.

2. Target Audience: (Who Is Your Ideal Customer?)
Have a picture of your ideal customer clearly spelt out. Create an 'avatar' for your ideal client. Be able to identify a real person out there who fits the image of your ideal client, and whenever you are marketing or speaking about your ideal customer, always bring the image of the person to mind. Then you would be able to answer questions such as: where he lives, shop, what he likes to eat and as much info as possible.

Using your 'avatar', write a target-audience profile based on demographics, including age, gender and any other important characteristic that will help you further understand the people you serve.

Of course, you probably have more than one type of customer buying, or that would buy your product or services. I am not saying you cannot sell to these other customers, however when it comes to devising a plan, it is wise and more productive to focus your message, lingo and other ideas around your most dominant target customer.

When you focus on a specific group of people, you are able to address their needs better and can create advertising messages tailored to suit them. It makes life easier and is cheaper than spending money on advertising to everybody. Your advertisement can focus on how your business solves a particular problem.

3.   **Goals: (What do you want to Accomplish?)**
What action do you want your ideal customer to take?

4.   **Strategies (How Can You Reach Your Target?)**
Now that you know who you want to reach and what actions you want them to take, you'll need to identify the best ways to reach them and with what message. This is simply what your strategy is all about. Your strategy should offer support and natural progression for your goal.

5 CORE STRATEGIES OF MARKETING PLAN

- Automated strategy: This happens whether you do anything or not. Example: Advertising, print advertising etc.
- Systematic: This is done periodically maybe weekly or monthly. Example: Blogging, email marketing etc.
- Expert driving mix: Whatever you do to set yourself as an expert because this will generate you income. Example: Speaking, seminar.
- Event based marketing: Live events, regular

webinar, teleseminar etc. to engage people and get them connected to you.
- Relational marketing: Done to build rapport, such as attending networking events. You need to build relationships with both customers and strategic partners.

All of these strategies, when properly executed, would definitely help you in making money and would also create the basis for your tactical and action plans.

In one of her webinars, Marlee Ward of Radical Entrepreneurship spoke about "How to create a highly successful marketing plan for your business." My interpretation and expansion on her lecture is detailed below. (I want to encourage you to check out her post. She is really awesome and has blessed me tremendously).

1. Ask yourself, what do you want to see happening in your business in let's say year 2015? Specifically, what are your goals? List them out. For example: Grow your email list by 500 subscribers; Book for yourself 3 speaking engagements.

2. Which of the items listed above (goals), if accomplished, will have the biggest impact on your business? Here you should select the best 3! Anything over 3 will distract and overwhelm you).

3. Based on your current schedule including school, work, family and maybe church, decide how many hours per week you can comfortable dedicate to working on each of these items to make it a reality. (This may include

networking, social media, blogging etc.).

4. Based on the available funds you have, how much money can you invest each month to make each of these priorities become a reality (this may include flier design and print, rental fees, banner and advertising).

5. What do you need to do to make your priorities (goals) a reality? Listed below are tactics that you could use to grow your business:

Networking
Speaking
Expos/tradeshows
Live events/workshops/seminars
Referral program
Building a referral program
Advertising-Print/Radio
Direct Mail-Postcard
PR Strategy/Press Release
Content marketing (blogging)
SEO
Facebook marketing
Twitter marketing
LinkedIn marketing
Pinterest
Video
Teleseminars
Webinars
JV Launches-online
Forum marketing
Banner marketing
Published case studies

Ensure you select the one you love to do, otherwise you will not do it or not do it well. Let it be a tactic you enjoy doing. Check all that applies to for one specific priority (Goal) Example: Sign up 15 new clients: networking, live event, SEO, Facebook marketing (you may select up to 10).

- Which 3 activities, out of the ones you selected, can you realistically cover, based on your TIME and BUDGET, and when will you execute? Working on 10 tactics are not realistic on one goal alone, so we will limit it to 3 that you can realistically do, based on your convenient schedule and funds. E.g. (Speaking to local networking group MONTHLY and Blogging-WEEKLY).

- List resources or action steps required to implement your 3 activities (tactics) above. Let us look at one (Action Steps) Example: Speaking to local networking group:

(Create Speaker 1 sheet, Pitch to group and create content calendar).

6. Repeat this process for all 3 objectives, which should come up to average of 9 tactics (activities), 3 for each goal and objectives. You can now engrain them into your daily activities, then marketing will become easy to implement.

7. Hold up, run a reality check and ask yourself these questions:

a) Have you allocated enough time to execute these projects?
b) Have you allocated enough money to execute these projects?
c) Do your activities cover the 5 core areas for effective marketing (automated, systematic, expert driven, event based, relational)?
e) Do you know exactly who you are targeting (could you tell me everything about them literarily)?
f) Are you clear and confident in your marketing message and positioning?
g) Can you clearly articulate the values and benefits of your services to your target market?
h) Do you know how to execute each of the activities you have chosen?

8. What will be your reward if you make all these happen next year? Think of a reward you will give to yourself if you can achieve your plans, and let this be visible where you can see it at all times. And if you eventually fulfill your plans, you should go ahead and fulfill your promise with the reward. It could be a vacation or a dress.

9. What one word reflects your desired outcome for next year? Think of one word that encompasses your overall desire for the year being planned for. It could be expansion or consolidation or any other word that best captures your desires.

10. Schedule it on your calendar. This is where your plans become feasible and broken down into daily, weekly and monthly actionable steps and activities

towards fulfilling your goals. Each of the activities, such as blogging, will now be transferred to your calendar with the dates and time visible for you to see. Also, both your number 8-(REWARD) and your number 9-(ONE WORD) should also be visibly written on your calendar, preferably at the top.

In Summary
- List your big vision goals
- Select your top 3
- Allocate time for marketing
- Allocate money for marketing
- Select 3 activities for each goal
- Repeat for goal 2 and 3
- Reality check
- Set rewards
- Set Reminders
- Put it all on your calendar

Are You Feeling a Bit Overwhelmed?
I know all of this may be too much for you to handle on your own, so I would like to invite you to join my Master Class on The Marketing Plan Boot Camp, which would not only help you simplify this process into practical easy to manage steps, but also help you answer additional questions about marketing budget, ideal target audience and many more. To sign up for this course, please register at http://gbengaomotayo.com.

14

LEVERAGING PR TO BUILD AWARENESS AND CREDIBILITY

"Can a rich man enter heaven?" Asa Candler, who was a very rich man, thought so. He accepted the principle of Christian stewardship, which holds that God gives wealth to individuals in order to promote His kingdom on earth. Candler thus felt obligated to protect and build the fortune that he held as a sacred trust, and to use it to carry out God's purposes in the world. - **Asa Candler, Co-Founder Coca Cola**

When a consumer sees third party coverage of a product or service, it is perceived much differently than a traditional advertisement. When we see an advertisement, we know the company is trying to sell us something. When a third party, such as the media, endorses a product or service, the company gains credibility. Consumers are much more likely to make a purchase based on third party endorsement than an advertisement.

A consistent public relations program will help build

general awareness of your product, service or brand and will supplement any direct marketing and advertising efforts. This visibility also tends to make your business appear larger and more established than it may be, which may help you secure partnerships, customers and funding.

What's the distinction between publicity and advertising? Advertising is what you pay for. Publicity is what you gain access to for free – oftentimes with the same outlets. Here are five things to take into consideration, when crafting a pitch for the media:

- Wrap your pitch around trendy topics/disasters – timing is key!
- Subject lines: Think TMZ...no boring: "Subject: How to be successful" email headlines.
- No attachments in your email, consider using hyperlinks.
- Less is more, don't be too wordy, 100 -150 words works: Headline >bullets> close!
- Be consistent & patient – the majority of your pitches won't get a response – but some will.

After someone has landed the media outlet they desired, how do they keep the momentum?

COMMON PR TOOLS AND TECHNIQUES

In order to build a relationship with the target audience and maintain it on a high level, PR specialists use a variety of tools and techniques. Some of the most common ones include:

1. **Attendance at public events:** In order to attract public attention and keep it engaged with a particular organization or an individual, PR specialists take an advantage of every public event and the opportunity to speak publicly. This enables them to directly reach the public attending the event and indirectly, a much larger audience.

2. **Press releases:** Information that is communicated as a part of the regular TV or/and radio programm, newspapers, magazines and other types of mainstream media achieves a much bigger impact than advertisements. This is due to the fact that most people consider such information more trustworthy and meaningful than paid ads. Press release is therefore one of the oldest and most effective PR tools.

3. **Newsletters:** Sending newsletters – relevant information about the organization or/and its products/services - directly to the target audience is also a common method to create and maintain a strong relationship with the public. Newsletters are also a common marketing strategy but PR specialists use it to share news and general information that may be of interest to the target audience, rather than merely promoting products/services.

4. **Blogging:** To reach the online audience, PR specialists use the digital forms of press releases and newsletters but they also use a variety of other tools, such as blogging and recently, micro blogging. It allows them to create and maintain a relationship with the target

audience as well as establish a two-way communication.

5. **Social Media Marketing:** Like its name suggests, it is used primarily by the marketing industry. Social media networks, however, are also utilized by a growing number of PR specialists to establish direct communication with the public, consumers, investors and other target groups.

15

FINDING A BUSINESS MENTOR

In the first months of opening your business, you'll need to make many important decisions. But you don't have to make every decision on your own. Ultimately, you're responsible for your business, but you can always consult a mentor for advice.

WHO IS A MENTOR?

A mentor is someone who has been down the same path you're taking. He or she is experienced, successful and willing to provide advice and guidance — for no real personal gain.

But how do you find a mentor? Here are some steps for finding and working with a mentor for your new small business venture.

GOVERNMENT-SPONSORED MENTOR ORGANIZATIONS

The government offers a great deal of free resources and services to support small business owners, both online and in person:

1. **SCORE Mentors:** Sponsored by SBA, SCORE provides free and confidential counseling, mentoring and advice to small business owners nationwide via a network of business executives, leaders and volunteers. You can connect with a SCORE volunteer in-person and/or online counseling.

2. **Small Business Development Centers:** SBDCs provide management assistance to current and prospective small business owners. SBDC services include financial counseling, marketing advice and management guidance. Some SBDCs provide specialized assistance with information technology, exporting or manufacturing. SBDCs are partnerships primarily between the government and colleges, administered by SBA.

3. **Women's Business Centers:** WBCs provides business training and counseling with the unique needs of women entrepreneurs in mind. WBCs are a national network of nearly 100 educational centers designed to support women who want to start and grow small businesses.

4. **Veteran's Business Outreach Centers:** VBOCs provide veterans with entrepreneurial development services, such as business training, counseling and mentoring.

5. **Minority Business Development Agency:** MBDA advisors help minority business owners gain access to capital, contracts, market research and general business consulting.

Additional federal counseling programs can be found on Business.USA.gov.

TRADE ASSOCIATIONS

Many trade associations operate mentor-protégé programs that provide guidance to help you build a business. These mentoring programs are often conducted through a combination of formal one-on-one mentoring sessions and group networking with fellow protégés. Business owners might be connected with multiple mentors for a more holistic experience.

Most industries are represented by trade associations, as are genders, ethnic groups and business types. If you need help finding a trade association, consult your local SBA district office.

MENTOR FOR GOVERNMENT CONTRACTORS

If your business plans to sell products and services to the federal government, you may need specialized mentorship. The General Services Administration (GSA) offers a Mentor-Protégé Program that is specifically designed to encourage prime contractors to help small businesses participate in government contracting. The SBA also has a Mentor-Protégé Program for small businesses.

LOOK TO YOUR NETWORK

Who do you know? Do you have a previous boss who inspired you or a friend who is a successful business owner? Ask that person to be your mentor, and learn from his or her advice and best practices. Just be prepared to share with them why you chose them in particular, your goals and what you are looking for from them.

WORKING WITH A MENTOR

If you decide to work with a mentoring organization, ensure there is a formal mentor-protégé structure in place. If you work with an individual, you'll need to establish a mutually beneficial, structured relationship. Remember these tips about mentoring:

- Be organized, prepared and consistent. Make sure you are respectful of your mentor's time.
- Do not expect your mentor to run your business for you or make decisions for you. You should have realistic expectations about what a mentor can provide you.
- Plan your mentoring sessions in advance. These could be as simple as having a one-on-one meeting once a month to discuss business goals, obstacles and regulatory requirements that you don't understand.
- Take notes, create action items and be prepared to review progress during your next session.
- Thank your mentor for his or her time and assistance with your business decision-making skills.

You are equipped with enough information to get started. We discussed how to overcome procrastination. It is now your time to move forward with wisdom and knowledge and to align yourself with those who God will link you to for your season of advancement. This is your time!

16

MARKETPLACE RESOURCES

"I never would have been able to tithe the first million dollars I ever made if I had not tithed my first salary, which was $1.50 per week." — **John D. Rockefeller sr.**

This chapter is dedicated to assist you in "advancing" in this season. We have taken the excuse from many of you who were "stuck" and did not know where to begin. Below, you will find pertinent information to get started, whether for ministry or business.

We thank **Mrs. Lavonya Jones** for providing much of this information to marketplace leaders.

TIPS FOR BUILDING YOUR PLATFORM

It doesn't matter what your business is or what industry you're in, these tools are absolutely imperative to your success in building a global platform. You can build a global platform from your home. You can be connected with people all over the world, just with your computer and an Internet connection. These tools can be automated and scheduled out in bulk. Here are some best practices for using online tools to build your platform:

- Share valuable content. Share content that your target market would be interested in, even if it is not your own content. Be discerning on what you provide for free and what you charge for.
- Separate your Facebook business page from your personal Facebook page.
- Post on social media three times per day - morning, afternoon, and evening. Share your most important content between the hours of 2pm – 6pm. It takes 7 times for a person to be exposed to your message before they consider buying.
- You can have an audio, video, or written blog. Blog twice per week - Monday and Thursday.
- Send your newsletter preferably once per week and share different content from what you share on your blog.
- Go to where your target customers are and provide value information to them by sharing your expertise: other blogs, forums, Facebook and LinkedIn groups, etc.

Newsletter
- Mail Chimp   www.mailchimp.com
- A Weber   www.aweber.com
- Constant Contact   www.constantcontact.com

Blogging
- Word Press.com   www.wordpress.com
- Word Press.org   www.wordpress.org

Radio
- Blog Talk Radio   www.blogtalkradio.com

- iTune   btr-tips/itunes-radio-show Magazine
- www.issuu.com
- www.joomag.com
- www.paper.li

Learn Best Practices from the Following Experts:

Tamyka Washington: tamykawashington.com
- Blogging and social media expert for women entrepreneurs.
- Offers free resources on starting a business with blogging.
- Low cost resources to help you launch a successful business and online platform.

Michael Hyatt: michaelhyatt.com
- Former CEO of Thomas Nelson Publishing.
- Offers many articles and podcasts on his blog to help you increase exposure for your platform.
- Provides WordPress and social media best practices.
- Has a book called "Platform" to help you learn everything you need to know to build an online platform.

Sandi Krakowski: arealchange.com
- Multi-million dollar online business and 100,000+ followers on social media.
- WordPress and Facebook expert.
- Offers free blogging course, Free E-Book, and over 60+ videos to help you be successful building your online business.

Linda Hollander: www.wealthybaglady.com
- Corporate Sponsorship expert.
- Learn how to get other businesses to fund your business and events.

MicroMentor.org: Get a free business mentor to help with any aspect of your business.

Free Online Business Resource Centers
- StartUp Nation
- Small Business Administration
- Quora
- BizLaunch
- WPMU Dev: For all things WordPress
- TED Talks
- Small Business Administration Learning Center
- Score Templates
- Slide Share

Freelance and Contracting Work
Work from Home Books by Connie Brentford
- Make Money Online: 97 Real Companies That Pay You to Work in Your Pajamas (purchase on Amazon)
- Make Money Online Vol. 2: 67 More Real Companies That Pay You to Work in Your Pajamas (Purchase on Amazon)
- Gig Salad http://www.gigsalad.com
- E-Lance http://elance.com/
- Fiverr http://fiverr.com

Free Web Conferencing Tools
- Free Conference Call

- Free Conferencing
- Anymeeting
- Twitter Chats
- Hootsuite
- Skype
- Google Analytics
- Microsoft PowerPoint
- Audacity
- Windows Live Movie Maker
- YouTube Downloader
- Animoto
- Screencast
- Buffer
- SocialOomph
- UserTesting

Instead of paying for expensive technology and equipment, you can use free and low-cost online tools to run your business and automate it to make money for you, while you sleep. It is also cheaper now to hire contractors to help you with your business. Whether you need help with logo design, website development, or technical support, it is much cheaper now to obtain those services. I hope that this information will provide the education and connection that you need to help take our entrepreneurial journey to the next level.

YOU ARE NOT MEANT TO HAVE A BOSS

Noted software engineer and venture capitalist **Paul Graham** goes so far as to say, "human beings aren't meant to work in large corporations." In his post, *You Aren't Meant to Have a Boss,* he makes this comparison: "I was in Africa last year and saw a lot of animals in the wild that I'd only seen in zoos before. It was remarkable how different they seemed. Particularly lions. Lions in the wild seem about ten times more alive. They're like different animals. I suspect that working for oneself feels better to humans in much the same way that living in the wild must feel better to a wide- ranging predator like a lion. Life in a zoo is easier, but it isn't the life they were designed for."

REFERENCES

1. Gary Vaynerchuk: Web 2.0 Keynote conference, New York (September 2008)
2. Dr. Jerry Savelle Seizing God Given opportunity.
3. Amos Johnson: Take Control of Your Financial Destiny
4. Marlee Ward: Radical entrepreneurship (www.marleeward.com)
5. Peter Weill: 2004 MIT study of 1000 largest US firms on the topic "Do Some Business Models Perform Better than Others?"
6. Seth Godin: Define: Brand (http://sethgodin.typepad.com/)
7. Callan Rush: (Prosperity Plan) in Magnetize Your Audience.
8. Chris Guillebeau: author of the $100 startup, "To succeed in a business project,
9. Pamela Slim: Escape from cubicle nation: from corporate prisoner to thriving entrepreneur
10. Sarah Pierce: Spirit of the Entrepreneur. http://www.entrepreneur.com/article/190986
11. Shannon Willoby: Fear https://blog.scottsmarketplace.com/fear-of-failure/
12. Guy Kawasaki: The Art of the Start.
13. Small Business Administration (SBA) www.sba.gov
14. Giants of God: http://www.giantsforgod.com/

ABOUT THE AUTHOR

Gbenga Omotayo is a 16-year veteran marketing and small business consultant, professional speaker, workshop facilitator, and event producer based in Brooklyn, New York. Gbenga is passionate about helping people discover, develop and deploy their God-inspired ideas into profitable ventures.

He helps people, ministries and businesses reach their highest personal and business potential. Gbenga has successfully managed major campaigns and projects for many faith based organizations.

As the CEO of Global Christian Event Network, he is the executive producer of the hit standup comedy show "Night of Gospel Laughs" and Christian Resources Expo. He has spoken on various topics with special emphasis on the areas of events marketing, marketing communications and business networking.

As the lead consultant and brands architect at Pacetas, a full service Digital Marketing Agency, his work is helping to transform countless ministries and small businesses in their approach to integrated marketing communications. Outside of work, Gbenga is the youth director at Abundant Life Christian Center and happily married with three great kids!

EXHIBITION | WORKSHOP | NETWORKING | MENTORSHIP
ACCOUNTABILTY PRAYING PARTNER

PLATFORM FOR SUCCESS
Iron Sharpening Iron
Prepare • Network • Promote

Bi-monthly networking event created to prepare, connect and promote christian entrepreneurs, business owners and aspiring ones across the tri-state.

Our platform is unique because it allows you to leverage FIVE powerful business tools:

- ✓ **PERSONAL RELATIONSHIPS**
- ✓ **BUSINESS EDUCATION**
- ✓ **MENTORSHIP SUPPORT**
- ✓ **PROMOTIONAL PLATFORM**
- ✓ **SPIRITUAL EMPOWERMENT**

To showcase/sponsor or RSVP:
info@GCENMedia.com | Tel: 917-826-3566
www.gcenmedia.com

PACETAS
A Full Service Marketing Agency

- 👤 Branding
- ✏️ Graphic Design
- ☁️ Website Development
- 🎥 Video Production
- 💬 Social Media Marketing
- ✉️ Email Marketing
- 📱 Mobile Marketing
- 🖥️ Digital Signage Advertising
- 📝 Event Marketing
- 👤 Independent Consulting

Tel: 917-826-3566
Email: info@Pacetas.com
Website: www.Pacetas.com

EASY TO IMPLEMENT MONEY MAKING MARKETING PLAN BOOTCAMP

Do you lack a written marketing plan?
Or have a plan that doesn't work?

THIS PROGRAM IS EXACTLY WHAT YOU NEED TO TURN THINGS AROUND.

IN THIS 4 WEEK PROGRAM YOU WILL LEARN:

1. The **single most important** factor in effective marketing and how to apply it to your business,
2. How to **find your ideal customers AND outsmart your competition,**
3. How much money is **TOO much money to spend** on marketing and advertising,
4. The **one thing you must do** for your marketing plan to work (and it's not what you've been told before).

DETAILS:

- 4 In-Depth Weekly Lessons that will Show You Exactly **How to Target the Right Prospects,** Complete **PRICELESS** Market Research, Set a Proper Budget, and Pick the **Best Marketing Tactics** for Your Business.

- 4 LIVE Coaching Calls to **Answer Your Specific Questions** and Provide Expert Guidance (valued at $2,220)

- One one-page Marketing Outline so You Have **Total Clarity** about Your Marketing -> **Because Clarity = Success**

- One downloadable PDF Execution Blueprint to Help You Create a Plan that **Makes You Money**

- Periodic **Feedback on Your Burning Questions** Via our Internal Comments Feature

- **Lifetime Membership** to The Platform for Success Entrepreneurship Workshop Library (and all it's perks!)

info@GCENMedia.com, (917) 826-3566, www.GbengaOmotayo.com/mplan

CONTACT ME

Congrats on completing reading my book. I hope it has helped you to get clarity about your God-given ideas, gifts and strengths and how to use them in starting your own business while employed.

For comments and one-on-one assistance: gbenga@gcenmedia.com

To sign up for my email newsletter with FREE tips, training and resources: www.gbengaomotayo.com

To book me for your group, event or program: (917) 826-3566. gbenga@gcenmedia.com

Until Next Time... BE INSPIRED TO SUCCEED!

Gbenga
@MeetGbenga

Printed in Great Britain
by Amazon